Always In Style

The Complete Guide for Creating Your Best Look

STYLE • BODYLINE • WARDROBE • COLOR • HAIR • MAKE-UP

Doris Pooser

THOMSON

COURSE TECHNOLOGY

Always In Style

DORIS POOSER

Fashion changes, but your personal style still reflects you. Are you more conservative or more dramatic? You can be appropriately dressed and <u>always in style</u> whatever your personal style preference.

Your Shape, Your Style

Select clothes that complement your body shape and reflect your personal style.

The proper shape guarantees proper fit.

Understanding your personal style assures confidence.

Always In Style

The Complete Guide for Creating Your Best Look

Always In Style was designed by Robert Hickey
Illustrations for the revised edition by Sachiko Kanai
Copy editing for the revised edition by Cathy Kreyche
Other illustrations from the first edition by April Reinking and Brenda Burkholder
Body and clothing diagrams by Christine Turner

Always In Style
  AIS Marketing Services
  347 Fifth Avenue, Suite 701
  New York, NY 10016
  TEL>212/696-1424
  FAX>212/696-1630

Trademarks
Course Technology is a division of Thomson Learning.
Crisp Publications is a trademark of Course Technology.

Disclaimer
Course Technology reserves the right to revise this publication and make changes from time to time in its content without notice.

ISBN 1-56052-413-8
Printed in United States by Banta
10 11 12 13 PM 06 05 04

ACKNOWLEDGMENTS

The following people have contributed to making this book possible and have continued to support the Always In Style concepts and programs.

Robert Hickey for his talent, organizational skills and on-going support.

Phyllis Avedon, my editor, for her ideas and way with words.

Rebecca Giles-Wiltshire and her husband Bill for their continued support, enthusiasm and endless wit.

Frances Wronski, my mother, for teaching me more about style than I ever realized.

Todd and Jeff Pooser, my two sons, for their support, love and encouragement.

Jim Pooser, my late husband, for encouraging me to start a new career with Always In Style.

To Jenny Hanson, Carol Spenser, Ulla Pallin and Akemi Sugawara, my international partners, whose talents and professionalism have enabled the Always In Style concepts to help women in Australia, the U.K., Sweden, and Japan.

To Michael Vaughn, the new man in my life, for giving me the opportunity to continue to expand my work and my life.

FOREWORD

To be well dressed, a women must wear clothes that complement her physically, express her personality, are current, and are appropriate for the occasion. She must develop her own style. Coco Chanel said years ago that style stays forever and fashion keeps changing. Both style and fashion are important. It is possible to use the very simple guidelines described in *Always In Style* to develop your own style and then to reach in the fashion direction that reflects your personality.

The popularity of the seasonal color system over the past number of years has led many women to begin looking for their "color." But many of them have become confused about where they "fit." One consultant may have identified you with one season, while another had a different "diagnosis."

Over the years I have worked with dermatologists, skin and hair labs, makeup labs, colorists and artists. For me this only confirmed the need to expand the original seasonal color system. My research shows that no one is all "warm" or all "cool." We are a combination of both in varying degrees, so a simple single seasonal palette is not enough. One palette may contain the greatest number of complementary colors for you, but all colors in that palette will not necessarily be suitable for you. The correct ones must be identified and other colors added from other palettes so that your individual palette fully enhances your unique combination of skin, eye and hair color.

This describes the Always In Style seasonal color system. *Always In Style* explains this system and, for the first time, confirms its validity with scientifically based facts.

In the revised color section, I will present new color palettes. You will be better able to recognize your most flattering colors, expand your color choices and learn to wear all colors in a unique and complementary way.

After the first edition of *Always In Style* was published, most new books on color presented variations on my expanded color system. Professional image consultants today use expanded color palettes. Most woman today realize the need for individuality and want and enjoy flexibility in their color and style choices.

Each year the shades and intensities of color available in clothing change. Always In Style was the first to recognize the importance of updating personal color palettes. These new colors, their color categories and the corresponding fashion themes are presented each season in the *Always In Style Portfolio*, a fashion publication available through AIS.

Fashion designers and experts from all over the world have expressed their enthusiasm about my concepts and agree that color is important. But it is only the "icing on the cake." Absolutely essential is to first select clothes that complement your body shape. Would you put the same red dress on Nancy Reagan and Elizabeth Taylor?

Of course not. But why? That is why I developed the Always In Style concept of body line.

Wearing clothes that complement your body size and shape is the most important element of style, so I have started out *Always In Style* with a description of body lines. Correctly identifying your body line will help you select clothing that looks like a natural extension of you.

Add the correct colors and you will have achieved the first step in identifying your style wearing clothes that complement you physically. Incorporate your personality and you can confidently say that you have found your own personal style.

I hope *Always In Style* will help those of you who have not yet discovered your style to develop it, appreciate it and enjoy it. Those of you who feel you already have your own style will be able to confirm why what you are doing works and will have additional confidence to reach further to be Always In Style.

CONTENTS

Personal Introduction

If Only...

"If only!" How many of you have an "if only" list? Mine was *long*. If only I were shorter, if only I didn't have such long arms and legs, if only my complexion were better, if only my face didn't happen to be so square, or if only I could look like my friend Mary.

I didn't just *say* "if only." I tried to *change* me. I frosted my hair to get rid of the red, contoured my jawline with dark foundation to make my face look oval, slouched to make myself look shorter, and spent years embarrassed about my complexion. I even tried to dress like my friend Mary. I tried to wear the silk blouses with soft bows that looked so wonderful on her. The harder I tried, the more frustrated I became. It's hard work trying to be something you're not—trying to look like someone else and knowing that it's impossible.

I finally decided to take a good look at myself, accept myself, and start over. I analyzed my body size and shape and compared it with others. I noticed the characteristics of clothing that complemented all of the different body types. After testing my observations on hundreds of others, I realized that each woman has her own individual style, which is determined by her unique body size and shape, her facial shape, her coloring, and finally her personality. You don't need to try to change any of these things. You *do* need to identify your unique characteristics and work with them.

I now accept and emphasize my square jawline, wear clothing that balances my long arms and legs, take advantage of my height, wear makeup and colors that complement my coloring, and save a fortune at the hairdressers, since I no longer change my hair color. *It is so much easier and so much more fun being me.* I also receive far more compliments. I now have my own individual style; it's very different from Mary's. I can enjoy her look without envying it because I now enjoy mine.

And that's what this book is all about: showing you how you can develop your own truly individual style.

Doris Pooser

PART I

STYLE

What is a Well-Dressed Woman?

Designer Coco Chanel first dressed her elegant clientele in suits in the 1930's. When Hollywood beckoned, her influence spread far beyond the couturier world. On screen and off, women began wearing suits. The "Chanel suit," which evolved during the fifties, has since become a classic.

The skirt is straight and elegantly simple. The short, collarless jacket has a straight, edge-to-edge closing. The simplicity and versatility of her design have made it internationally popular—available in all price ranges, in all colors and fabrics. To be "well-dressed" has often been simply a matter of wearing a Chanel suit.

And then there's the basic black dress, with a plain jewel or scoop neckline, a straight skirt and fitted waist, and long or short sleeves, depending on the season. The little black dress has been a tradition for generations. It has also been a social necessity—essential to own,

The Chanel suit continues year after year. Skirt and jacket lengths rise and fall, shoulders may broaden and colors reflect the season and time, but the basic style remains a classic. Updated versions can be boxy or emphasize the waist, making the style more versatile.

Always
In
Style

13

regardless of how you looked in it. Your were always "well-dressed" in your basic black.

Our casual lives have also been strongly influenced by the fashion industry. A case in point: the seen-everywhere "alligator" shirt made famous by tennis star Rene LaCoste. Although it has spawned look-alikes bearing polo players, horses, and foxes, many men -- and women-- continue to rely on the alligator shirt to keep them safely well-dressed on the sports scene.

The corporate women of the seventies was expected to emulate her male counterparts--navy pin stripes, tailored bloused, and minimal makeup were the well-dressed business woman's uniform of the day.

Today, however, women are less willing to conform, either to the expectations of the corporate world or do the dictates of designers.

A matter of balance

Today's well-dressed woman thinks in terms of the total picture she creates. This include her makeup, clothing and the way she carries herself. To fully express who she is, the colors, designs, fabrics and details involved must all balance with her coloring, her body size and shape and her facial features. These factors must also balance with who she is internally, which is reflected in the way she moves and walks. This non-verbal message, which comprises 55 percent of what she says to others about herself, is essential to her style.

This all-important balance is created when what you are wearing looks like a natural extension of you by complementing your characteristics as well as your personality. How can we accomplish this? Few of us, especially since grew up with the security of "dedicated" styles, were taught what to look for when selecting our clothing. Instead, we learned to shop sales, or to buy looked nice on our friends. Consequently we never succeeded in defining our individual style, let alone relating it to the clothes we should wear.

Some lucky souls can put on an article of clothing and instinctively know it creates the balance and harmony that make it right for them. The styles they choose always seem "theirs," and they have a knack for mixing pieces and accessories to create interesting, exciting looks. They're the ones envied for their natural flair for fashion.

Many of those on today's best-dressed lists are there because they have this innate ability to select the right clothing. Others make these lists because they can afford personal shoppers or have found one or two designers whose clothing consistently works for them. Although these women are fortunate in that they have been able to develop their style, they too can benefit from understanding why the clothes they wear work so well for them. It is always fascinating and exciting to learn the "whys," and to learn to perfect what you already know.

But those of us who have not been blessed with a natural flair for style—who have not yet managed to reach best-dressed status—*can* acquire the skills that it takes to get there. The list is less important than the satisfaction of knowing that you qualify. When you as an individual reach your maximum potential—when you always look as wonderful as you can—it will be because you have discovered your individual style and how to put it to work for you.

Every one of us wants to look good, to feel good about ourselves, to look youthful and up-to-date. Whether we shop in Paris or buy our clothes in our local department store or boutique, we can all look fabulous. How? By knowing what to look for when we select our clothes.

Beginning the Search for Style

Dramatic, Classic, Elegant, Chic, or Just You?

Today's designers offer us a bewildering array of styles from which to choose. With so many options, deciding on the ones that are best for us can be a real problem.

Many recent books have defined categories of styles to help those struggling to find their own special look. Carole Jackson, author of the best-selling *Color Me Beautiful*, classifies styles as Dramatic, Classic, Natural, and Romantic. In *Dressing To Win*, Robert Pante categorizes women as Glamorous, Elegant, Spicy, and Chic. These categories are ideal starting points. They have helped make us aware of the differences in styles and encouraged us to search for that one special, perfect style. I spent years believing that when I finally arrived at a specific style and classification, it would answer all of my questions and meet all of my needs. I analyzed each of the different categories, hoping to find the one that ideally suited me.

I have always felt classic and formal, preferring clothing with a traditional cut. Yet the

Classic, Dramatic, Romantic or Natural? Real style doesn't necessarily have a tag. Today's fashions mix fabrics, shapes and styles. This allows you to create your own style with your own tag.

classic Chanel jacket, pin-striped suit, and shirtwaist dress made me feel and look out-of-proportion—awkward and rather ordinary. This was an incredibly frustrating aspect of searching for my style since it can be such an elegant look on the right person. But even though the traditional classic styles didn't seem to work for my body size and shape, I was determined not to give up the search for my own classic look.

Many people have called my style Natural because I like texture and wear it well. Yet I have never been comfortable in informal clothes and rarely, if ever, go without my makeup, even on my day off. I look better in a plaid or tweed jacket than in an all-plaid suit, which is too heavy and bulky for me. My facial features and bone structure cannot take the weightiness of a tartan plaid or a stacked-heel walking shoe. More importantly, I do not enjoy a Natural's informal lifestyle.

I have also been called Romantic. I love movement and softness in my clothing and have a long willowy body that allows me to wear clingy fabrics. However, I am not comfortable in glitter, flounces, laces, or chiffon. I prefer tailored styles, even for my dressy looks.

I have often had the desire to be Dramatic. I am tall and fairly slender, but do not have dramatic coloring or strong, exotic features. I love to follow the latest fashion trends and enjoy trying new fashion looks. Even though I felt it would be fun and exciting to wear certain exaggerated styles, in the past I lacked the confidence to try them. I was never sure where "high fashion" ended and "trendy" began!

Robert Pante, in one of his "salons," described me as elegant and glamorous. Was that because of the way I dressed, carried myself, and moved, or was it because of the role in which he saw me that day? Doesn't everyone want to feel glamorous at some time during their life? I must admit that I don't feel terribly glamorous sitting at my typewriter at 10:00 at night, but I do still have my makeup on. Perhaps I am glamorous at heart.

The more I studied the different categories of styles, the more I realized that none of them really described *me*. In addition, coming from a generation that tended to have seasonal styles dictated to them, I really wanted more flexibility than they seemed to offer. I also wanted to know how to wear *more* than one style.

Our lifestyles today make it important for us to be able to wear many different styles, depending on the occasion, not to mention our moods and our need for excitement and change. By expanding the definitions of the categories, we can end the search for a single style and consider several. Let's stop for a moment to look at these expanded definitions.

A **Dramatic** person is often described as tall and slim, with vivid coloring, angular features, and a certain sophistication. Does that mean that someone who's five-foot-two can't look dramatic?

Absolutely not! It all depends on how you define "dramatic." I have always considered dramatic to be a high-fashion look that anyone can wear, regardless of her size and shape, if she truly has the desire for this look and understands the rules of dressing. Many petite women look marvelous in ultra high-fashion clothes. Actress Susan Lucci, who has appeared in leading fashion magazines, graces the popular soap opera "All My Children" with a fabulous dramatic look. Diminutive Susan always looks wonderful in her dramatic clothes.

Many tall, slim, angular women just don't look right in a high-fashion look and would never feel comfortable dressed that way. The off-stage Carol Burnett is a perfect example. She is obviously comfortable in conservative clothing, and has given priority to her desires, feelings, and personality in selecting clothing. When dramatic is defined as an extreme in line and design, we realize that very few people are able to dress in a dramatic style while looking and feeling appropriate for all occasions. Cher is one of the few who can wear extremes and obviously feel comfortable in them. Bob Mackie, who designs clothing for both Carol Burnett and Cher, has been able to create styles that are appropriate for both by considering their physical characteristics and personalities as well as their likes and dislikes.

In the study of style, extremes are rarely considered good fashion. Let's define Dramatic, then, as a high-fashion look that is tastefully done and can be worn by anyone, regardless of her size and shape, once she understands what to look for when selecting her individual clothing styles. Because this look is not appropriate for all occasions, it's important to expand your knowledge of styles so that you know where and when a particular style can be used effectively.

A **Classic** is often thought of as being of medium height with even, well-balanced features; someone who is well-proportioned and has a relatively conservative outlook on life. But what about the person who is well-balanced, well-proportioned, of medium height, who *isn't* conservative, or at least is conservative only part of the time? She should not be limited by a particular style in which she is not really comfortable. And those of us who are not necessarily well-proportioned, and who are taller or shorter than average, sometimes want or need a classic conservative look.

Today's corporate woman has made great strides away from her conventional "uniform." Women in the business world now feel freer to dress in ways that express their individuality. Career achievements can mean even greater flexibility in clothing choices, but a conservative air remains important; her flair for fashion should never overshadow a woman's professional skills. Surveys confirm that certain colors and looks promote her credibility and enhance the power look. Her status as an equal among men dressed in conservative business suits is improved when she wears a suit or jacketed dress. Navy blue, brown, camel, and gray increase credibility and should therefore be an integral part of a corporate wardrobe. There have been significant changes in recent years, but it is still necessary and wise to dress conservatively in a corporate setting.

My definition of Classic, therefore, is a conservative look that everyone has a need for, depending on the occasion. Some people are naturally more conservative than others, and will want to use this look more often. Each of us, however, regardless of size and shape, should have her own version of the Classic look.

Does **Romantic** mean ruffles, glitter, and high-heeled shoes? Yes, at times. But everyone can have her own romantic look if we think of Romantic as an outfit and mood for a quiet evening at home with a special someone. Each of us would wear something different to achieve a personal romantic mood. Jane Fonda, Nancy Reagan, and Joan Collins would each dress differently, translating "romantic" according to her individual style. Joan Collins might wear a black charmeuse dressing gown trimmed in black lace. Jane Fonda might choose a silk smoking jacket with a shawl collar and silk trousers. Nancy Reagan might don an elegant ivory caftan with a mandarin collar. Romantic means different looks to different women. Some like glitter and heels, and love being "dressed up." These perennial romantics may have to work at not looking overdressed in their daily lives.

The word **Natural** conjures up thoughts of someone tall, with a sturdy or athletic build, who is casual and enjoys informality. Yet many people are born with large bones and sturdy builds but feel very formal and conservative. (Or they like to be dressed up all the time, or are mad about the dramatic look.) As we've pointed out, body size and shape alone should never dictate style. Everyone likes a casual, informal look at certain times. Most working women appreciate the opportunity to escape from the need to get "dressed" in the morning, or to have to apply their usual makeup. But those who tend to rely on the casual look (and whose lifestyles suit this way of dressing) must be wary of the times and places when they need a more professional or business look.

In classifying styles, it is important to realize that we are describing many things. The words dramatic, classic, natural, and romantic evoke thoughts of occasions, moods, and personalities as well as overall impressions of types of clothing that would be appropriate for these times and places. Unfortunately, these "overall impressions" are not sufficient.

One of my colleagues once commented that she was analyzed as a Summer, a Classic, and Spicy. She sent out a plea to her friends to help her find a Summer's blue, soft Classic, Spicy dress. Using this description would not only complicate the search, it would produce a wide range of dresses, depending on who did the choosing.

As you can see, these kinds of labels do not give us specific information about actual pieces of clothing and how they should relate to us personally. They can, however, be used effectively for describing times, places, and personalities. There are times and places for all looks and it is necessary to know when to wear each of the styles. The appropriateness of dressing for the occasion cannot be overemphasized. The Appropriate Occasions chart explains some of the times and places for wearing different styles.

Appropriate Occasions for each Style

	Dramatic	*Classic*	*Natural*	*Romantic*
Work	Entertainment	Corporations	Teachers	Not Appropriate
	Fashion Industry	Law, Medicine	Child Care Workers	
	Department Store Buyers	Politics	Work involving physical labor	
	Boutique Owners	Government Employees	Work not dealing with public	
	Art-related Industries	Social Workers	Service-oriented professions	
	Interior Designers	Teachers	Grocery and variety store personnel	
	Advertising	Real Estate		
	Media-related professions	Politicians		
	Public Relations dealing with above			
Casual / Leisure Time	Sports events	Church functions	Sports events	Candlelight dinner
	Picnics	School meetings	Picnics	Evening at home
	Shopping	Civic events	Recreational activities	
	Recreational activities	Board meetings	Shopping	
	Relaxing	Political gatherings	Gardening	
			Relaxing	

Chart continues on next page.

	Dramatic	Classic	Natural	Romantic
Social and Obligatory Events	Cocktail parties	Cocktail parties	Resorts	Cocktail parties
	Dinner parties	Dinner parties	Vacation areas	Dinner parties
	Movies	Theatre—only when dressy top, jewelry, shoes, and bags are added to conservative suits and work clothing	Family-style restaurants	Dances
	Weddings			Theatre
	Lectures, if group is young and related to one of the above work areas			Weddings
				Formal occasions
		Funerals		
		Lectures		
		Speeches		
		Presentations		

Note: Those who are self-employed have considerable flexibility in determining what is appropriate. The deciding factor should be their audience and/or the people they will be dealing with. To dress 'appropriately' means that you will look successful and credible, but will not intimidate or make others feel uncomfortable.

Knowing who you are

Once you've established your guidelines for appropriateness, it's important to consider your likes and dislikes and your personality. Each of you, because of who you are, will tend to be most comfortable with one or two styles. This is fine when the occasion offers a choice. You must, however, learn to appreciate the need for different looks. As you gain confidence in understanding how your clothing relates to you, you will be surprised at your new interest in different types of clothes. You will then be able to dress in a manner that fully describes who you are as a person.

No matter how precisely a style is defined it still doesn't tell us what to look for when selecting clothing to be worn on a specific figure. Classifications are interesting, fun, and informative, but in order to use them to develop your individual style, you must first understand what they mean with respect to your individual physical characteristics. It is important, therefore, to learn some basic rules about the construction of your clothing and how it relates to your figure's requirements. When you have these parameters within which to work, you can learn to dress in exactly what is right for you.

Before I learned the guidelines and how to relate clothing construction to my body, I spent many a sleepless night worrying about what I would wear for that special event. I can remember piles of discarded outfits on my bedroom chair as I frantically searched for the one that looked right. I hate to admit it but I have had days and evenings ruined because I didn't feel right in the outfit I finally selected and didn't know why. Now that I have a practical and easy set of guidelines to tell me what to look for in selecting my clothing, I always feel good about the way I look and have the time and energy to devote to more important matters.

In order to define and determine your own individual style, it is important to look at your physical characteristics. You were born with a particular body type and special facial features. When you find the appropriate clothes to complement all of your positive characteristics you can reach and stretch in the fashion direction that makes you feel most comfortable. Once you understand your physical characteristics you will be able to develop your style and flair by combining the line, designs, fabrics, scale, and colors that complement your special qualities. You can then create wonderful and unique combinations that reflect your personality and creativity.

Style:
A Definition

Which characteristics of clothing determine its style? Let's consider three parameters—line, scale, and color—and how each of these directly relates to your physical characteristics. Keep in mind that your clothing should be in balance and harmony with your body size and shape and your facial features. It should look as though it belongs on you, and is a natural extension of you. The line of your clothing—the silhouette line—should complement the line of your body. The amount of texture and any patterns you wear should be in direct proportion to this line. The scale of your clothing should be proportionate to your body size. And, of course, the colors you wear should complement your natural coloring.

As I take you step by step through line, scale, and color, you will learn how to analyze yourself to determine exactly what to look for when shopping for clothes. You must be honest with yourself and be able to look at yourself objectively. You were born with a special body size and shape as well as special facial features. You may wish you were shorter, taller, thinner, or whatever, but

Whatever your shape or size, you can select clothing that looks like it was custom made for you. Patterns, fabrics, prints and accessories will all work together, creating the right balance and harmony.

wishful thinking has no place here. You must accept yourself; accept what you have been given and make it work for you. You'll discover your limitations (everyone has them), but you will learn to work *around* them to play up your positives. You'll learn to turn the things you once thought of as faults into assets. You'll also find a new joy in being you as you reach to create exciting new looks that you never dreamed of before.

Q. *I have always been described as a Classic. I am well-proportioned, have an average build, and am shy. I am ready for a change. How can I change my look for the better?*

A. A classic tends to be conservative or to prefer a conservative way of dressing. You are obviously ready to be less conservative. When you find your correct body line and scale, you will be able to wear many different styles, depending on your mood and the occasion. As you gain confidence with your new look you will be able to reach for many variations. You do not have to start with an extreme; reach slowly in your new fashion direction. Try a new length skirt, a new big top or jacket. If you like it and are comfortable, reach a little further. Use your new guidelines to help you break out of your ultra-conservative style.

Q. *I have been told that I am a Natural. But I'm not athletic and feel very romantic and soft inside. How can I be me inside and out and still look right? What is my right style?*

A. No one needs to be limited to a single style of dressing. Look again at your physical characteristics as well as your personality and lifestyle. Once you truly understand your best lines, fabrics, designs, and colors, you will be able to develop your own distinctive style.

Discovering Your Body Line

Let's begin by describing line as it relates to you as an individual. When determining the best style to complement a particular body we need to analyze which body characteristics can be related to the corresponding characteristics of a piece of clothing.

Your physical characteristics are tangible and readily identifiable. How do you describe your body? Your facial features? Words like tall, short, thin, wide, broad, round, curved, or straight relate to a body type as *a type of line*.

A line is an infinite number of points with a direction. The direction can be straight or curved. Body silhouettes and facial shapes are often described as being diamond, square, rectangular, oval, pear, heart, round, or some combination of these. *Each of these shapes can be defined by either a straight or a curved line.* The diamond, triangle, square, and rectangle are created with straight lines. The oval, round, heart, and pear are created with curved lines.

Once you understand your bodyline, you can select clothing that compliments your positive characteristics and corrects any minor figure flaws.

The first step: analyzing the direction of the line of your body and of your facial shape and features. Will it be straight or curved? Your predominant overall characteristics—your body as well as your face—will be defined best by one of the following geometric figures: triangle, square, rectangle, ellipse, oval, or circle.

It is possible to see the silhouette of your body by looking at your shadow. Stand several feet from a solid, smooth wall. Face the wall and shine a light from behind you. Your shadow will be visible on the wall in front of you. Your silhouette line will be predominantly straight or curved. A predominant line can also be seen by looking at your body shape from a distance. Stand back and look at yourself in a full-length mirror. Some of you will see straightness, others will see curves. Some of you will find it difficult to identify the dominant line because suggestions of both straight and curved lines will appear. It is best to see your outline when looking at yourself in something like a leotard so that you see the silhouette of your body without being distracted by details.

Let's look first at those body shapes that have predominantly straight lines. These body types are often tall and thin, with small, flat hips, broad shoulders, small busts, and very few curves. Others in this category, though not especially tall or thin, have flat hips, square shoulders, and square or rectangular bodies. Remember, weight is not a factor here. We are looking at the silhouette line, not at height or weight.

If you find it difficult to determine your body line, look at your facial shape. The initial line impression that we get when looking at someone is often determined by their facial shape and features. "Straight" facial features are angular. A long slender nose, high cheekbones, a square or pointed jawline, and diamond or rectangular face shapes tend to create straight lines. Some straight lines on body types and facial shapes appear very sharp and straight, almost extreme; others are straight but less exaggerated. The sharper lines are best described by diamond and triangular shapes, the straight by square and rectangular shapes. In each case the body line and facial line can be described by

Straight-line body types

Look carefully at the examples of straight-line body types:

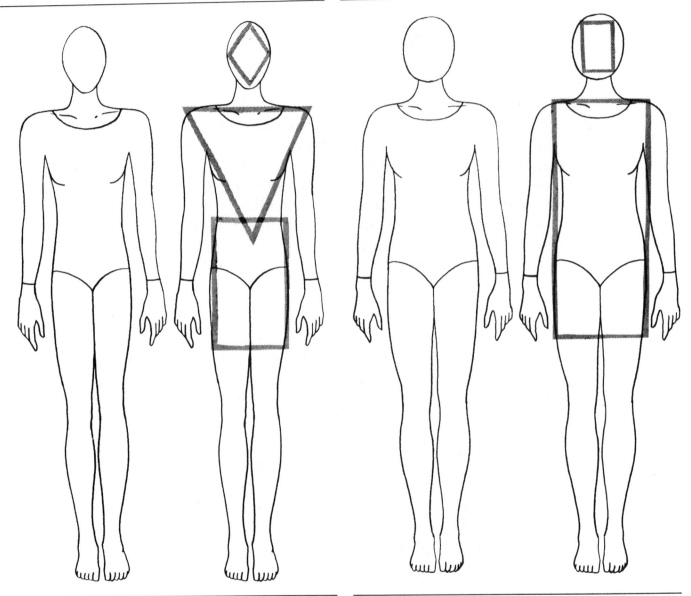

Sharp-Straight   *Straight*

Notice how the geometric overlays emphasize the basic shape of each body.

a straight line. One is a "sharp-straight" line; the other is a "straight" line. Do not let one prominent characteristic, such as a full bust, or large hips or thighs, distract you. Focus on the overall impact of facial features and silhouette line.

Those of you who have curved body-lines will have either soft smooth curves or obviously rounded curves. Your body silhouettes will appear rounded, with curved hips, shaped waists, and full busts.

Your facial shape will be oval, round, heart, or pear. You may have rounded cheeks, full lips, and round or almond-shaped eyes. These body shapes can also be described as round, oval, heart, or pear. In each case, the curved line can generally be described as oval or circle, depending on the degree of curve.

Rounded body types

Look carefully at the examples of rounded body types:

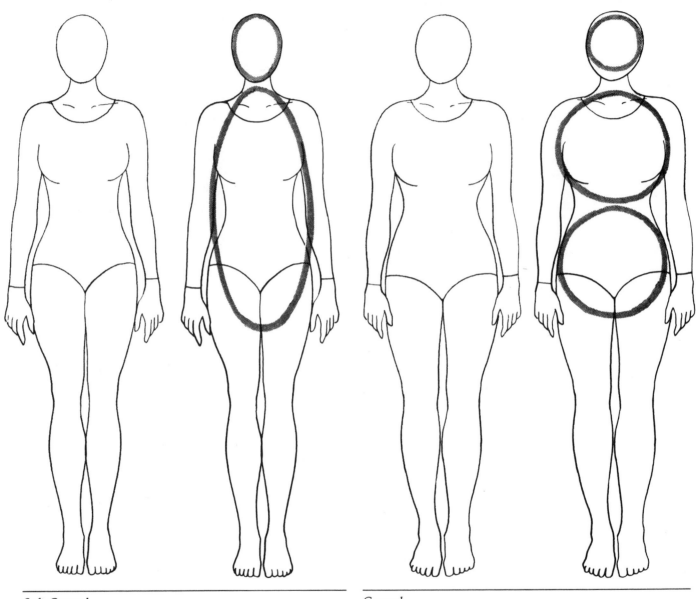

Soft-Curved

Curved

Notice how the geometric overlays emphasize the basic shape of each body.

If your "straightness" or curves are not obvious to you, your body line is probably best described as a combination of straight and curved lines. A tall person's body curves may not be readily apparent because her height accentuates the feeling of a straight line. The result is a softened straight line. You need not be tall, however, to have a soft-straight line.

The effect of a soft-straight line can also be seen in those whose facial "line" contrasts with their silhouette line. Curved facial features with a straight body, or a slightly curved body with straight facial features, combine to create the appearance of a soft-straight line. These straight facial features often have some softened edges that create a balance of straight and curved lines. The ellipse, or elongated oval, best describes this body type. If you are having difficulty determining your body line, you may well have a "soft-straight" body line.

Soft-straight body types

Look carefully at the examples of the two types of soft-straight bodies:

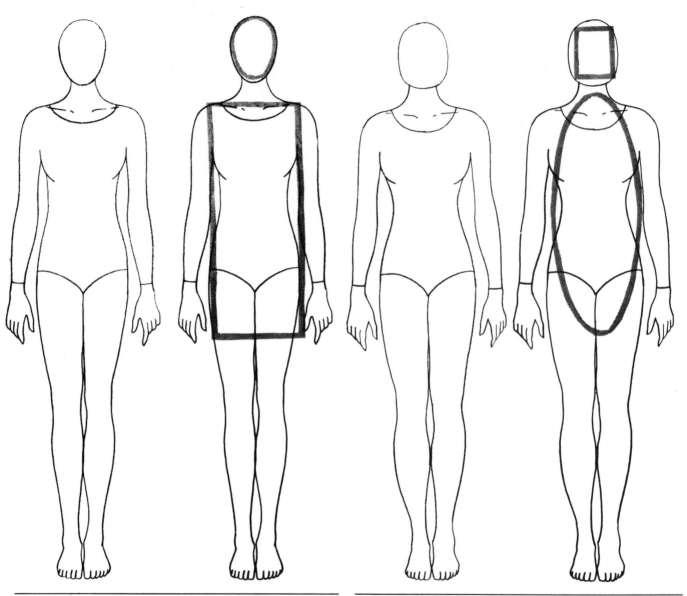

Soft-Straight

Soft-Straight

Notice how the geometric overlays emphasize the basic shape of each body.

Q. *Whenever I borrow my roommate's blazer, I look older and feel stuffed into it, even though we wear the same size. Why?*

A. Blazers usually have straight lines, sharp lapels, and square details. You most likely need curved lines in your clothing. Look for shawl collars, slightly fitted waists, and curved details on your jacket. You can still achieve a wonderful classic look that will complement your body by wearing lines that are right for you.

Q. *I always admire lovely silk flowers pinned to a lapel or tucked behind an ear for evening. Every time I try this look, I feel ridiculous, like an aging Carmen Miranda.*

A. You most likely have angular features and straight lines to your body. Clothing and accessories with straight lines will look more balanced for you. Try a wonderful geometric pin on your lapel or a silk scarf with an abstract design tucked into your pocket.

Whether you are tall or short, slim or heavy, you will be able to describe your facial shape and body silhouette in terms of line, either straight or curved. It doesn't matter how straight or how curved, it's the overall impression that counts.

Look at these body figures, lined up from the straightest to the most curved. See the gradual movement from one body type to the next? Remember, there are many variations in between, since everyone has a unique and different body shape.

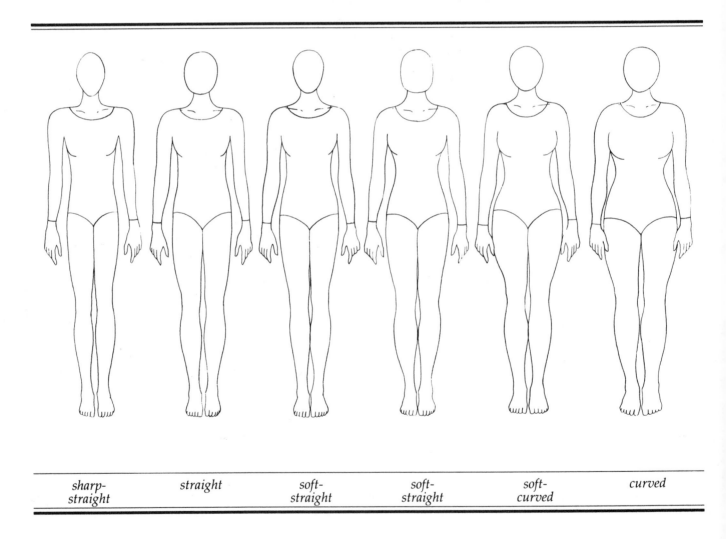

| sharp-straight | straight | soft-straight | soft-straight | soft-curved | curved |

This chart describes facial and body shapes in terms of lines and geometric figures:

Body Lines

	Sharp-Straight	*Straight*	*Soft-Straight*
Face Shape	diamond square triangle	square rectangle oval (with square jaw)	oval ellipse
Body Shape	inverted triangle (broad shoulders) rectangle or some combination with the triangle	square rectangle	rectangle with slight curve
Overall	triangle (broad shoulders) angular face, straight body	rectangle	ellipse with the slight beginning of a curve
Figure with Overlay			

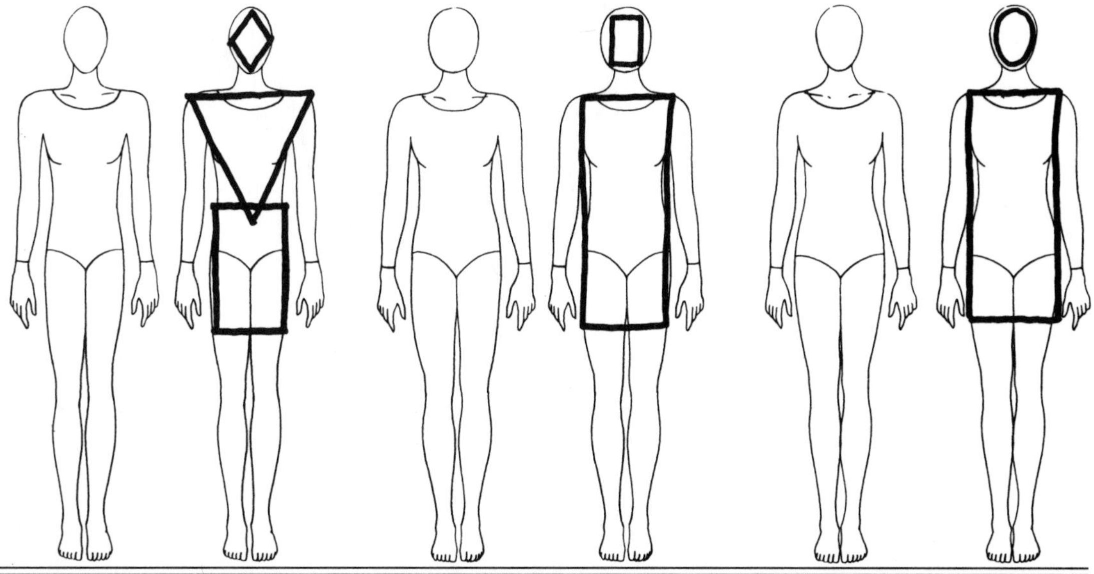

Sharp-Straight   *Straight*   *Straight-Soft*

	Soft-Straight II	Soft-Curved	Curved
Face Shape	square soft edges on square or rectangle	oval round	round oval
Body Shape	ellipse	ellipse oval	oval or round
Overall	ellipse, slightly rounded curved	oval and defined curve	round, very curved voluptuous body
Figure with Overlay			

Straight-Soft   Soft-Curved   Curved

Where Do You Belong on the Graph?

If you are still having difficulty determining what your exact facial and body lines are, don't worry. We are simply looking for the predominant line that best describes the first impression of your physical characteristics. There is a continuous, gradual transition from the sharpest and straightest line to the softest and most curved. As individuals, each of us has a different and unique body line that can be classified somewhere from sharp-straight to curved, depending on the predominant line we project. There's no need to select an exact point on the line graph or become overly concerned about whether your body is sharp-straight or just straight. It is enough to know that you're in the straight range instead of the curved or vice-versa. You'll note that facial-shape and body-shape categories overlap in the charts of geometric shapes.

It's interesting to get a small group of people together and line them up in order, from the one who has the straightest silhouette and facial shape to the one who has the most curved. You will see a number of subtle variations. Even though several of you may have straight body lines, each will look different. Some lines will be sharper than others and some will probably fit into the soft-straight range. The purpose of lining up is to show the continuum of different body types.

For our purposes you need only find the *area* that describes your body size and shape. Elizabeth Taylor would be a *C,* Nancy Reagan would be a *B,* and Cher would be an *A.*

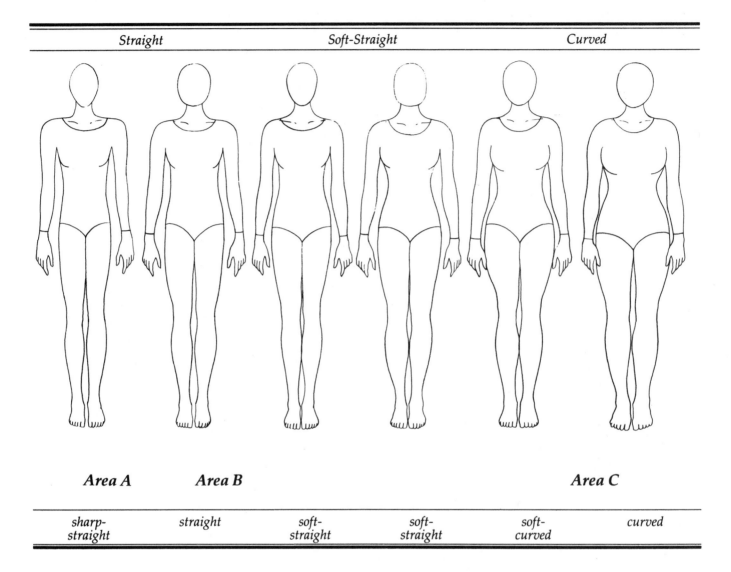

Straight		Soft-Straight		Curved	
Area A	**Area B**			**Area C**	
sharp-straight	straight	soft-straight	soft-straight	soft-curved	curved

Notice that a straight body line can be very sharp and straight or lean toward soft-straight; the body line would still be defined as "straight." Soft-straight body lines may lean toward either straight or curved but will be considered "soft-straight." Both soft-curved and curved body lines may be considered "curved" for the sake of simplicity. We are therefore considering three basic types of body lines; straight, soft-straight, and curved.

Consider the following examples of well-known people with different body lines:

- **Sharp-Straight**
  Cher   Nancy Kissinger
  Pat Buckley   Diane Von Furstenberg

- **Straight**
  Nancy Reagan   Geraldine Ferraro
  Katharine Hepburn   Jacqueline Onassis

- **Soft-Straight**
  Jane Fonda   Princess Diana
  Linda Evans   Farrah Fawcett

- **Soft-Curved**
  Ann Margret   Linda Carter
  Jaclyn Smith   Joan Collins

- **Curved**
  Elizabeth Taylor   Dolly Parton
  Zsa Zsa Gabor   Beverly Sills

Some of you will have more flexibility in describing the line of your body because your characteristics are not extreme or exaggerated. Because the two extremes—sharp-straight and curved—are sharply defined, they are the easiest to identify. When the line is less well defined, the range is of course broader. But even those in the soft-straight range will see a **direction** of either straighter or more curved.

Degree of Flexibility

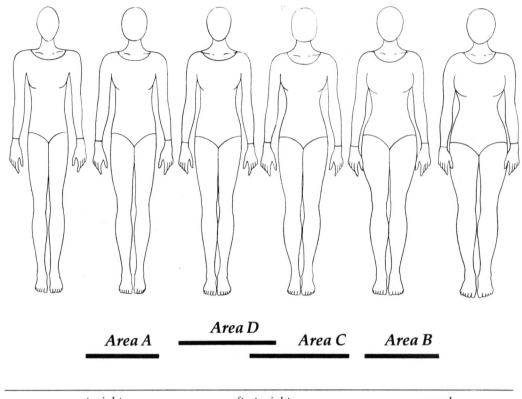

Area A   **Area D**   **Area C**   **Area B**

straight   soft-straight   curved

Area A describes a body type with predominantly straight lines. It doesn't matter how straight; you simply fit in the straight range.

Area B describes a curved body. Regardless of the degree of curve, you can describe your range as curved.

Area C describes a soft-straight line which, because it is less well defined than either straight or curved, includes more body types. However, the direction of this range is toward curved.

Area D describes a soft-straight body whose direction is toward straight.

Moving along the continuum

As we leave our teenage years and move on through our twenties, thirties, and ensuing decades, we rarely retain the same body shapes. As we add weight to our frames, our body line tends to soften, as does our facial shape. Grace Kelly, as a young movie star, had soft-straight lines in her face and body. As she matured, Princess Grace of Monaco moved across the graph to a soft-curved line. Think back to your teens or twenties and you may notice a comparable progression for your body along the line graph. Although you may notice a movement from sharp-straight to straight, from soft-straight to soft-curved, or from soft-curved to curved, you will *not* see a movement from one end of the graph to the other. The bone structure and features you were born with, which are part of you, will always be present. Learn to recognize them and make them the foundation of your personal style.

Clothing as an Extension of You

Throughout history there has been enormous variation in the body line chosen as the personification of beauty. In the days of the ancient Egyptians, the tall, slender body and angular face were considered the ideal. Deities were always represented by these figures. During the development of western civilization, the curved, rounded body was held to be the height of beauty. The ultra thin has periodically been in vogue, as was the case during the "Twiggy" era. In today's fashion world the tall, slender, slightly curved body, with an oval face, is looked upon as the perfect combination.

Whatever body is "in," we are bombarded with information teaching us how to camouflage the bodies we have. When tall and thin is in we are told to cover the curves with straight lines. Straight and vertical lines do create length. A straight dress with a center seam does look longer than a dress with no seam. But how does it look on a curved body? It covers the curves, of course, but looks stiff and totally unrelated to the body beneath. There is an obvious separation between the

It is when your clothing looks like a natural extension of you that you look your best. The shape, proportion, fit and color must all complement you. Most important, you must feel comfortable with your style.

clothing and the wearer; balance and harmony are missing. In order for clothing to be complementary, there must be a relationship between it and your body so that the clothing becomes a natural extension of you.

Imagine Elizabeth Taylor in a straight skirt and long, straight double-breasted jacket with sharp lapels. Why does this not present a balanced image? She needs clothing with soft, contoured lines to balance and complement the curves of her body. A soft wool crepe suit with a slightly flared or eased skirt, a short jacket with rounded lapels and slightly fitted waist would complement her figure. Cher, by contrast, would look wonderful in the straight skirt and jacket because it would complement her straight body shape and angular face.

Fortunately, today's woman has no need to change or camouflage her body whenever a new "ideal" emerges. She can instead work with her body line to emphasize its beauty. How much easier it is being ourselves, instead of trying frantically to change what we have. When we know we look our best we can enjoy being ourselves. And it is so much more comfortable!

The joy of being comfortable

I use the word "comfortable" frequently in my classes and lectures. In the movie *Same Time Next Year*, Alan Alda asks Ellen Burstyn to leave her husband for him. In spite of a long, less-than-perfect marriage, she declines. She says that her marriage is "comfortable." I often reflect on the meaning of comfortable as it was used in that movie and as it applies to our lives. Acceptance, security, satisfaction, belonging, and lack of pretense are all part of being comfortable. Being "comfortable" with our style is just one part of being comfortable with ourselves and our lives.

Too short to be "perfect"?

By working with your body lines when selecting clothing you will not emphasize over- (or under-) weight problems because you will be working with the right line, fabric, print, and texture for you. And accept your height. Why wear an unflattering dress so that you can seem an inch taller? Learn to wear the right lines and proportions to look fabulous and no one will think twice about your height.

So many articles have been written on how the short person can look taller. For example, she has been told to wear self-fabric belts to create a continuous line in her dress. I have almost never seen a self-fabric belt on a dress that didn't cheapen it. I prefer to add a contrasting leather belt or tie. Even if you are short, you can wear a contrasting belt lower on the waist, or wear hose and shoes the same color as your skirt hem to create a finished look. The positive addition of the wonderful belt will far outweigh the potentially negative effect of wearing the wrong belt in order to look taller. If you are short, accept it. Don't spend your life wishing you were tall and trying to look just a little taller by wearing unflattering styles. There are too many wonderful looks for you to have fun with to bother trying to change your height.

Saying no to the ideal oval

Just as the "ideal" body has been promoted, so has the perfect oval face. We have been conditioned to strive for an oval face, and to make ours more so with the aid of makeup and hairstyles. How boring for everyone to be walking around with an "almost" oval face! An oval face is wonderful for the person who was born with it. The rest of us need to capitalize on the face shapes we have. Whatever the shape of your face, it helps make a statement of who you are. It is you. Play up the wonderful angles, emphasize the curves.

The most harmonious and most flattering clothing for your body will have the same line as your body and face shape. Don't try to change your shape—enhance it! Let's look at the clothing lines that will help you develop a successful personal style by working *with* your body line, not against it.

PART III

YOUR CLOTHING

Which Clothing Line is Yours?

There are several lines to consider when looking at any item of cloth-ing. One line is the silhouette line—the cut or exterior line of the garment. As with body lines, some articles of clothing have very sharp exterior lines and some have very curved lines, with all degrees of straightness and softness in between. Let's start with the sharpest, straightest clothing lines and go on to the most curved.

The sharp lines of the outfit in the illustration labeled *Sharp-Straight* are reflected in its strong angles; in the large, well-defined shoulders,

| *Sharp-Straight* | *Straight* |

closings, and hemlines as compared with the less exaggerated straight lines in the illustration labeled *Straight*.

Continuing across the spectrum we have what I refer to as the soft-straight-lined garment. A soft-straight line is achieved by using exterior construction lines that are smooth and soft with relatively little curve, or by using straight lines with a loose unconstructed fit and/or with a softly woven fabric. The looser construction provides a soft feeling without creating obvious curves. Here are two types of soft-straight-lined garments:

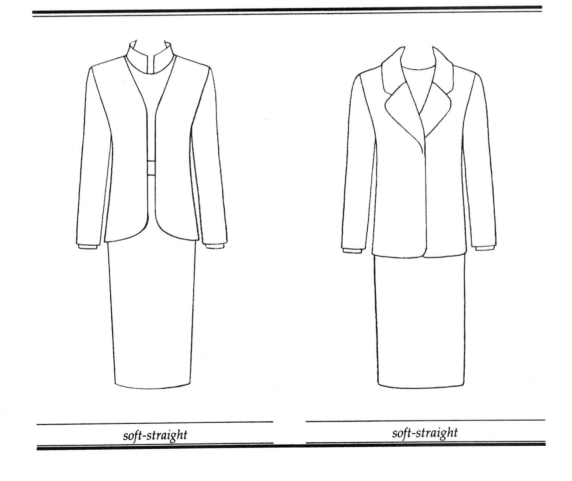

soft-straight   *soft-straight*

Next let's look at clothing with soft-curved and curved exterior lines. Notice the roundness and softness of the line. Curves are created by the garment's cut and shape, as shown in these figures:

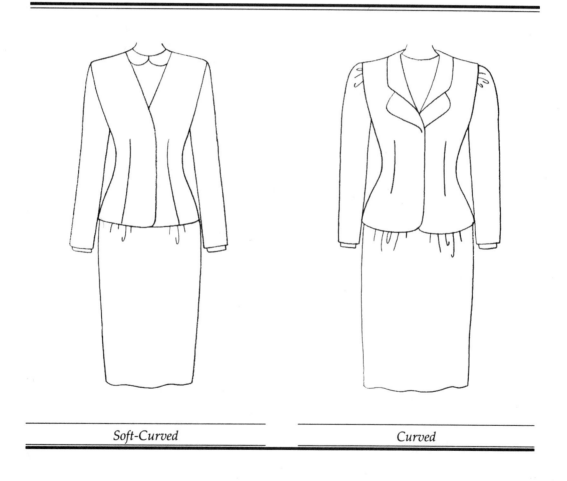

| Soft-Curved | Curved |

Types of clothing can be placed on a line graph in the same manner as different types of bodies. Thousands of types of silhouettes can be placed along the line. Keep the idea of a continuum in mind—not a limited number of individual categories.

It is the overall impression created by the outline, the flow, and the design of the garment that determines the predominant external line characteristics. You should be able to identify a general straight line, a curved line, or the in-between soft-straight line.

Choose your clothing line:

| sharp-straight | straight | soft-straight
soft-straight I | straight-soft
soft-straight II | soft-curved | curved |

*I am *not* suggesting extremes—using circles on round bodies and severe lines on straight bodies. It is only necessary to think in terms of tailored, straight, or crisp at one end and a movement to contoured, curved, or softened at the other end of the spectrum. Complement the line of your body by using similar lines in your clothing.

Identifying
Detail
Lines

Detail lines emphasize and balance the total look of a piece of clothing. Many details can define a specific line. Those details that create a straight line should be used on clothing that has straight silhouette lines. Details that emphasize curves should be used with curved silhouettes.

For soft-straight silhouettes it is possible to use straight details as long as the overall impression of the finished piece has a soft flow to it. This can be achieved by use of a soft fabric or by using a single straight line in a garment when the remaining portion of the garment is soft in fit and line. An exaggerated straight line in the skirt can be offset by a cowl neck or shawl collar on the blouse. It is also possible to use some curved details, such as a round collar, yoke, or pocket, as long as the end result is not totally curved. An unconstructed jacket or straight pleated skirt will balance these curves. Overall, softened straight lines result from softened lines or a combination of straight and curved lines.

The details that best describe each line type are shown in the following pages.

Details reenforce shape and style. Pleating, tucks, contrasting trim, button placement and even shoe detail add accents that create interest and contribute to the overall fashion statement.

Detail Lines

	Straight Lines	Soft-Straight Lines	Curved Lines
Darts	long straight darts	straight or pleated	soft gathers instead of darts
	sharply defined or no darts		soft pleats instead of darts
			eased
Seams	well-defined seam lines	straight with unconstructed look	small seams
	top-stitching		curved seams
	contrasting piping, braid or trim	self top-stitching	no top-stitching
			fine top-stitching
			eased
Pleats	pressed down	pressed down with soft fabric	soft
	stitched down		unpressed
	asymmetrical	unpressed	gathered
			eased
Sleeves	set-in	set-in	gathered
	straight pleat at shoulder	raglan	eased
	square shoulder-pads	dolman	drop shoulder
	tapered sleeves	slightly padded shoulders	raglan
	crisp puff	rounded shoulder-pads	soft
			full and billowy
			rounded shoulder-pads

Detail Lines *(continued)*

	Straight Lines	*Soft-Straight Lines*	*Curved Lines*
Lapels	very sharp	notched with soft fabrics	rounded
	notched	shawl	curved
	straight with interfacing	sloping	shawl
	pointed	rounded	bias
	peaked	sharp or peaked with soft fabric	
Collars	pointed	straight with soft fabric	round
	notched	rolled	rolled
	straight with interfacing	cowl	cowl
	square	notched	notched with round edges
	stand-up		
	piped		
Pockets	well-defined	patch with rounded bottom	flap
	square	slash	rounded
	piped	flap	set-in
	slashed	square with soft fabric	
Jacket	edge-to-edge closing	self trim	slightly fitted
	square hemline	subtly defined waist	well-defined waist
	fitted or loose	loose	rounded bottom
	asymmetrical closing	unconstructed	curved closing
	contrasting buttons and trim		
Necklines	square	boat	round
	boat	curve	scoop
	jewel	turtle	draped
	contrasting trim	scoop	flounce
	V	V	ruffled
	mandarin	cowl	cowl

	Straight Lines	*Soft-Straight Lines*	*Curved Lines*
Lapels	very sharp	notched with soft fabrics	rounded
	notched	shawl	curved
	straight with interfacing	sloping	shawl
	pointed	rounded	bias
	peaked	sharp or peaked with soft fabric	
Collars	pointed	straight with soft fabric	round
	notched	rolled	rolled
	straight with interfacing	cowl	cowl
	square	notched	notched with round edges
	stand-up		
	piped		
Pockets	well-defined	patch with rounded bottom	flap
	square	slash	rounded
	piped	flap	set-in
	slashed	square with soft fabric	
Jacket	edge-to-edge closing	self trim	slightly fitted
	square hemline	subtly defined waist	well-defined waist
	fitted or loose	loose	rounded bottom
	asymmetrical closing	unconstructed	curved closing
	contrasting buttons and trim		
Necklines	square	boat	round
	boat	curve	scoop
	jewel	turtle	draped
	contrasting trim	scoop	flounce
	V	V	ruffled
	mandarin	cowl	cowl

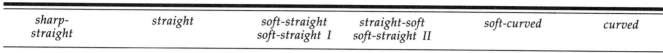

sharp- straight	straight	soft-straight soft-straight I	straight-soft soft-straight II	soft-curved	curved

Body lines:

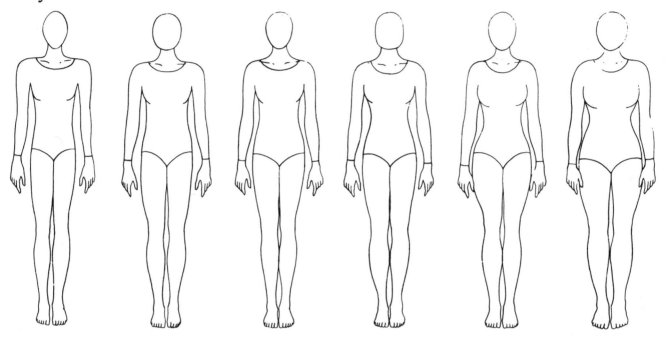

Clothing lines:

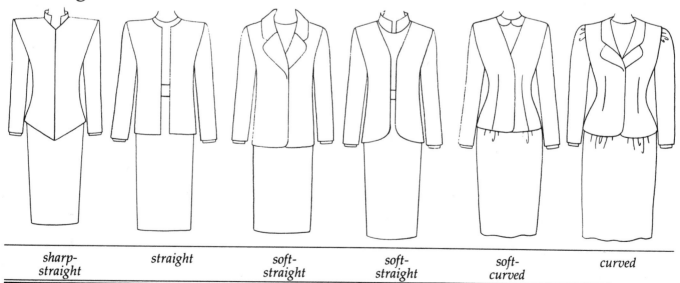

sharp- straight	straight	soft- straight	soft- straight	soft- curved	curved

Characteristics that Affect Clothing Lines

Fabric Weight

In looking at fabrics, it is important to consider weight, design, and texture, since they too affect the direction of the line. A line in geometry has only one dimension. But since we're using it as a fashion term, I am going to add other dimensions to help describe some of the characteristics of clothing and how they should balance with your special body characteristics.

Beyond the single dimension of a line—its length, including its direction—it is important to consider what I call the second dimension: the width of the line. When purchasing a pen, you have to decide what kind of point you want. Pen points range from fine to "standard" to broad. Consider the same jacket, drawn with both a fine-tipped pen and a broad-tipped one.

One looks lighter and finer; the other looks heavier and bulkier. What makes a garment seem to be defined by a fine line or a broad line, and who would wear each? This width must be considered for balance when we look at your bone size and your facial features.

Some of you have fine, delicate facial features and are small-boned regardless of your weight. You need a fine line in the construction of your clothes to keep them from looking too heavy or bulky for your structure. How do we create a fine line in clothing? By using fine top-stitching, stitching close to the edge of the garment, or no top-stitching; fine, small buttons, trim, and details; and fine fabrics such as wool crepe, fine gabardine, fine broadcloth, silk, chiffon, boucles, and hand-kerchief linen. Whatever the fabric, it should not be bulky or heavy.

Some of you have bigger bones, and larger and stronger facial features. Larger bones give you larger wrists, ankles, legs, and so on. These are not faults or problems unless you make them stand out or exaggerate them by wearing clothes with too fine a line. The balance would then be lost and you would overpower your clothes. You need the jacket drawn with the broad-tipped pen. How do you create this feeling? With heavier top-stitching, saddle-stitching, and stitching that is double-spaced or a machine-foot away from the edge of the garment; heavier and larger buttons, accessories, and details; and fabric such as wool flannel, medium to heavy gabardine, tweeds, linens, raw silks, satins, knits, and similar fabrics. Avoid those that are light or delicate.

Those of you who have neither exceptionally fine features and small bones nor large bones and facial features will have greater flexibility in your fabric selection. Remember, however, you are looking for balance. Select fabrics that are neither too heavy nor too light for your frame. The traditional silks, cottons, wools, and linens come in all weights. The medium weight is best for you. Gabardine, challis, jerseys, and satins are all good choices in medium-weight fabrics. Be sure that your details, trim, and buttons are neither too small nor too large for a totally balanced look.

During President Kennedy's term of office, his wife Jacqueline made an enormous impact on the American public. Her classic suits and pillbox hats made a fashion statement that women everywhere wanted to emulate. Her style was correct for her body line. However, some of the fabrics she used were too fine for her bone structure and broad face-shape. Wool flannel or medium gabardine would have been more complementary to her stature than her choice of wool crepe. Heavy satin is a better choice for her Romantic look than gossamer chiffon.

To determine whether you have small, medium, or large bones and facial features, look at these charts:

Facial Features

	Fine	Average	Broad
Nose	Slender, narrow small, thin	in between in between	Broad, wide, flat strong, hook, large
Lips	well-defined, narrow small, thin	in between in between	full, round, large
Mouth	small, delicate	in between	large, full
Eyes	small, almond	in between	round, large, angular
Jawbone (from under ear to center of chin)	5"	5" to 6"	6" or more

Bone Size

	Wrist measurement	Ankle measurement
small bones	5½" or less	8" or less
medium	5½" to 6"	8" to 9"
large	6" or more	9" or more

Texture

Textured fabric may be described as rough, nubby, or loosely woven. It is the line's third "dimension"—its depth. The depth of the fabric affects the direction of the line as well as the width. Look at this picture of the same jacket shown with and without texture. Notice that the line is softened by the use of texture at the same time that bulk is added.

Examples of two jackets with and without texture.

Loosely woven or highly textured fabrics create softer shapes. Edges and corners appear diffused and more rounded.

Crisp, tightly woven fabrics create straighter lines. Corners, edges and details appear sharp and clean.

People often ask me, "Can everyone wear texture?" I tell them that this question has a number of different responses. Designers often relate texture to size and color. They frequently use more texture with muted and monochromatic colors to create interest. When we consider only color and size, we ignore the impact that texture has on line. It is important to think about how texture affects the direction of clothing lines.

It is very difficult to create sharp lines with a loose, nubby, or textured fabric. If you need a sharp line to your clothing to complement the straight line of your body, you should use little or no texture. Sharp-straight lines work best with tightly woven fabrics such as wool gabardine, sharkskin, or linen, or fabrics with a sheen, such as silk, charmeuse, and taffeta. The most texture that can be worn to effectively create a sharp line would be fine linen, Thai silk, or tightly woven twill or tweed. The use of stiff interfacing can help to achieve a sharp line with a fabric that would otherwise drape or fall softly, as can braid or trim.

Those of you whose bodies are in the curved category will find that texture does not work well. Texture will make your curves look bulky and bumpy instead of smooth and sleek, and will make you look overweight (the typical teddy-bear look). Soft, flat fabrics drape well and fall in the soft folds that are so necessary for a curved line. Fabrics such as silks, wool crepes, jerseys, challis, and wool and silk blends are all appropriate.

For those who need a soft-straight line, texture is wonderful. It was made to create the exact line you need. Any softly woven fabric with texture automatically falls into soft straight lines without creating curves. This does not mean that the person who needs soft-straight lines must wear only textured fabrics. She can wear all types of fabrics, including the smooth and shiny ones, as long as she uses the weight that corresponds to her bone size.

When you look at the graph, notice the use of texture with respect to the direction of the line. Those who need the soft-straight line can wear the most texture; less and less is used as you move out to the two extremes of sharp-straight and curved clothing.

Texture

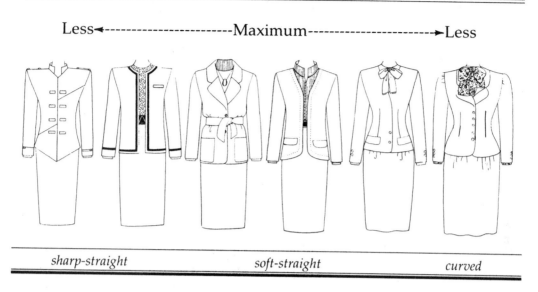

Less◄----------------------Maximum----------------------►Less

| sharp-straight | soft-straight | curved |

Print

The final relationship to line—the fourth "dimension"—is the print of the fabric. Prints, like texture, work best when used *with* the line of the garment rather than against it. From time to time designers assault our esthetic senses with prints that might best be described as vivid imagery. Bold cabbage roses and wild Hawaiian prints on tailored tops seem to emerge successfully every four or five years. They sell like hotcakes in the stores, but only for a season—as long as the fun fad lasts. Good style, by contrast, dictates that the line of the print be in tune with the line of the garment, thus creating an elegant and appropriate coordination.

The sharper and straighter your body line, the more geometric or "sharp" the print you wear should be. Soft floral prints used in sharply tailored styles do not create a balanced look. Those who need soft, curved lines are better in soft prints and watercolors. A contoured, soft feeling in the print as well as in the construction is essential to total balance. Those who can wear soft-straight lines need designs that are neither too straight nor too curved, and that allow for the movement and flexibility of the line. Here, too, they will have some flexibility in their selection of prints, since a geometric print will often be softened just enough by a soft-straight construction.

Notice the categories of prints:

- **Straight**

Geometric	Check
Stripe	Houndstooth
Abstract	Aztec pattern
Modern	
Sharp plaid	

- **Soft-Straight**

Paisley	Realistic
Stripe	Jungle
Plaid	Check
Animal motif	Tweed

- **Curved**

Floral	Paisley
Watercolor	Swirl
Realistic	Scroll
Rounded	

Taking exception

There are a few exceptions to note in terms of the relationship between print pattern and garment line. For example, if the line is strong and well-defined, the print pattern may vary a bit from the line. A small geometric print can often be incorporated into a soft-curved line. A stripe or plaid on the bias will be softened and will often work for a softer line. This combination may not be perfect, but is more acceptable than the reverse, a floral print made into a tailored style. The soft-straight line at times may combine a floral skirt with a straight jacket to create an overall impression of a softened line.

As a general rule, straight prints may be used in soft-straight or curved construction if, and only if, the construction is well-defined. Line and texture should be considered first; then print.

Twill Stripe

Stripe

Tartan Plaid

Foulard

Bouclé

Tweed

Linen

Floral

Houndstooth Plaid

Paisley

Houndstooth Check

The Lines Designers Use

As I describe clothing and its "lines," details, construction, fabrication, and quality, I will use the work of some of the leading international fashion designers as examples. These designers set the trends for each season and provide a direction for all of us. Most use a specific line when creating their collections, which makes it possible for us to compare these lines as they relate to our body lines. Few of us can afford to buy these creations, just as few of us can afford a painting by Picasso or Monet. We can, however, learn a great deal from them as we become aware of what to look for with respect to line, quality, design, and scale. And even though these designers may be out of reach for you financially, NEVER pass up an opportunity to try on these designs—to familiarize yourself with the fit and feel of perfection. Observe designer collections in fashion magazines and in boutiques and department store displays. You will gain a reference point and a guide to help identify lines in more affordable price ranges.

Some designers prefer straighter shapes and designs, other more curved. Some use a mixture. This simple shape with slight waist emphasis works well for many body shapes and is often used by Calvin Klein, Episode, Evan Picone and Anne Klein.

The moderate-priced designers and manufacturers often use a favorite line, but are more likely to incorporate several different lines into their collections. They do this because they look to many of the major international designers for ideas and trends, and most importantly because they are appealing to a larger and more diversified market.

Here is a list of the major international designers with the lines they tend to use most frequently. I have also included the moderate-priced designers and manufacturers with the lines seen frequently in these collections. Remember, you will be able to find several lines in their collections, which makes it particularly important to begin to recognize the different body lines in clothing construction.

International Designers

- **Straight lines**

  Adolfo
  Chanel
  St. John
  Andre Laug
  Yves St. Laurent*
  Carolina Herrera

  Louis Feraud
  Castleberry
  Mary McFadden
  Gucci

- **Soft-Straight**

  Perry Ellis
  Calvin Klein
  Bill Blass
  Giorgio Armani
  Donna Karan

  Issey Miyake
  Yohji Yamamoto
  Escada
  Gianni Versace

- **Curved**

  Halston
  Zandra Rhodes
  Valentino*
  Emanuel Ungaro

  Oscar de la Renta*
  Betty Hansen
  Hanae Mori

*Often use extremes of both straight and curved lines

Moderate-Priced Designers and Manufacturers

- **Straight**

Geiger
Pendleton
Albert Nipon Sport
Jones of New York

J. G. Hook
Evan Picone
Stanley Blacker
Schrader Sport
Kasper for J. L. Sport

- **Soft-Straight**

Carol Little
Anne Klein II
Perry Ellis Portfolio
Geoffrey Beene Sport
Adrienne Vittadini

Liz Claiborne
Calvin Klein Classifications
Willie Wear
St. Tropez
Blassport
Anne Pinkerton

- **Curved**

Tahari
Norma Kamali
Christian Dior
Ellen Tracy

Prophecy
Flora Kung
Ralph Lauren
Cloak of Many Colors
Marc d'Alcy

Nancy, Jane, and Liz know their lines. Have you learned yours?

Nancy Reagan has straight-line body and facial features. She needs straight crisp lines in her clothing and can wear many of the straight-line designers' clothing well. Jane Fonda needs a soft-straight line to create balance and harmony for her. She will fare best in the soft-straight lines of the designers listed in that category. Elizabeth Taylor will be her most ravishing in clothing from designers who favor a curved line in their collections.

Nancy Reagan's wardrobe has been in the news time and time again. Everyone interested in fashion knows by now that Adolfo is one of her favorite designers. Interestingly, whether she is aware of it or not, she understands her body line very well. Adolfo designs tend to have very straight lines and details, and a minimum of texture.

In January of '85, Mrs. Reagan appeared on the cover of *Time* magazine in a red dress with soft lines. Two weeks later she was again photographed in a red dress, this time in the straight-lined dress with standup collar that she wore for her husband's inaugural speech. The difference in her appearance was stunning. As one observer pointed out in a later "letter to the editor," the first dress "looked like it came from K-Mart." She may have chosen the dress to make her look more approachable—more like "middle America," but how sad! That's hardly the look we hope for, whether we shop at K-Mart or Saks Fifth Avenue. Remember, once you find your right line you will be on your way to looking successful, credible, and fabulous. *It isn't how much you spend on your clothing, but how knowledgeable you are in selecting what is right for you.*

When I completed my study of body and clothing lines, I was finally able to understand why that Chanel jacket, pinstriped suit, and shirtwaist dress looked wrong on me. Each of these pieces has a very straight line. In order to complement my body and facial features, I needed a soft-straight line in my clothing. The straight-lined clothing looked stiff and rigid instead of like a natural extension of me. But— and this is an important "but"—I did not have to give up my suit, my tailored jacket, or my classic shirtwaist dress. I now shop for a jacket with a slightly curved edge, a shirtwaist dress with a shawl collar, and a suit in a soft tweed instead of a pin stripe.

Now that you know the direction of your line (straight or curved) to use in selecting your clothing, the width of your line (fine to broad), the depth of your line (the amount of texture), and the print design, let's look at the Clothing Lines chart, which summarizes this information. Also included for your reference is a Fabric Types chart.

Fabric Types

- *Bouclé*—A slightly nubby wool or wool blend knit fabric. The surface finish has small loops or curls.

- *Broadcloth*—A tightly woven smooth fabric, usually of cotton or cotton blends.

- *Challis*—soft, light-to-medium-weight fabric with a diagonal twill-like weave. It is made in wool, cotton, rayon, or a blend.

- *Chiffon*—a sheer, lightweight, flowing fabric, usually in silk or silk blend, which drapes well.

- *Crepe*—a lightweight fabric of silk, wool, or blend with a slightly raised or finely puckered surface. The surface creates a matte finish.

- *Crepe de Chine*—a soft, lightweight crepe of silk or silk-blend fabric with a slightly raised surface. The surface has a matte finish.

- *Flannel*—a cotton or wool fabric that is medium to heavy in weight with a slightly fuzzy and matte surface. The fuzzy and soft surface makes the fabric moderately soft.

- *Gabardine*—a tightly woven diagonal twill weave that comes in all weights. It is generally a wool or wool blend but may be found in cotton. Because of the tight weave it is stiffer than a flannel.

- *Jersey*—a soft fine knit of cotton, wool, or blend that has a matte finish and falls softly.

- *Linen*—a fabric with a defined weave because of the sturdy threads. It comes in all weights. It tends to be stiff unless used on the bias or in flared styles; the lightest weight is called handkerchief linen.

Clothing Lines

Line width	Straight	Soft-Straight	Curved
Fine	lightweight fabrics that are stiff	lightweight fabrics that fall softly	lightweight, flat, fine fabric
	top-stitching at edge	loosely woven	fine, small buttons and details
	tightly woven fabric	small, buttons, details, and trim	fabrics that drape
	small buttons, details, and trim	top-stitching at edge	top-stitching at edge
Average	average-weight fabrics, stiff, crisp, and tightly woven	average-weight fabric woven to fall in soft straight lines	average-weight fabrics that drape easily
	average-size detail and trims	average-size buttons and trim	average-size buttons and detail
	well defined top-stitching	top-stitching; not at edge, subtly defined	no top-stitching
			top-stitching on edge
Broad	medium-to-heavy-weight fabrics, stiff and tightly woven	heavy, loosely woven fabric	medium-weight fabric
	large buttons, trims, and detail	large buttons, trim, and detail	large details and trim
	double or large top-stitching	double top-stitching	no top-stitching
Texture	little to none	maximum amount	little or none

Clothing Lines (*continued*)

Line width	Straight	Soft-Straight	Curved
Fabric Type	gabardine	linen	crepe
	linen	Thai silk	challis
	twill	challis	raw silk
	silk	tweed	jersey
	Thai silk	satin	chiffon
	taffeta	jersey	satin
	satin	wool flannel	
	moire	raw silk	
	polished cotton		
	pique		
Prints	geometric	paisley	floral
	abstract	plaid	watercolor
	modern	animal motif	realistic
	sharp plaid	realistic	rounded
	check	natural scene	swirl
	houndstooth	check	scroll
	herringbone	tweed	

Let's Talk About Scale (and Proper Fit)

Now that you have selected the best line for your clothing, including the right print and correct amount of texture, it's time to consider the next characteristic of style, which is scale. Scale can make the difference between looking elegant, sophisticated, and fashionable, and looking ordinary. Even though you may not be ready for high fashion, you should strive for a fashionable and current look.

Wherever I travel in the world, I notice that European women tend to look well-dressed and elegant. Their clothing invariably looks beautiful—superbly tailored and well-balanced. They seem to understand proportion, and have traditionally preferred quality to quantity. They look for quality in fabric, construction, design, and fit. One quality silk blouse, they would insist, is a hundred times better than five inexpensive imitations. These women understand that clothes must be what I call expensively or elegantly loose.

Some years, styles are big and loose. Other years they are tight and body hugging. Good style is always projected with an elegantly loose fit and quality construction.

American women are the biggest offenders when it comes to preferring quantity over quality. For some reason we have the misconception that we need an extensive wardrobe to look well-dressed. How can we possibly wear the same blouse to the office twice in one week? This way of thinking about fashion, however, is nonsense! It is far better to wear the same beautiful blouse every other day as long as it makes you look and feel great than to wear a different one each day of the week in which you feel and look ordinary.

There are several things to look for in a well-made, quality piece of clothing. Here are points to check when selecting clothing:

Quality Construction

- **Seams**
  inside seam allowance should at be least ⅝"
  seams should be finished with zig-zag or clean finished
  seam line should not pull or wrinkle but should "hang straight"
  no thread should be loose
  exterior stitching should be even, straight with no loose threads

- **Interfacing and facings**
  should not wrinkle, gap, or pull
  should be sewn in rather than fused
  inside facings should have top-stitching or be on bias

- **Hemlines**
  must hang evenly and straight
  must be finished with tape or clean finished on edge
  stitching must be loose and should not pull
  stitching should not be visible

- **Pockets**
  must be straight
  must be clean finished
  must lie flat

- **Buttons and buttonholes**
  buttons should be bone, leather, or covered (replace plastic buttons)
  buttonholes should not have loose threads
  tailor-made buttonholes must be straight

- **Belts**
  replace self-fabric belts with leather or woven belts
  do not use plastic belts; one neutral leather belt is better than any plastic

- **Thread**
  color must match exactly
  should not be clear plastic
  thread should be same type as fabric

- **Jackets**
  should be fully or half-lined if wool
  bottom hem should be straight
  collar should lie flat
  collar and lapel edges should lie flat, not buckle or curl
  top-stitching must be even

- **Fabrics**
  prints and plaids must be matched at all seams
  fabrics should be natural or blends that look like natural fabric

Small is (not necessarily) beautiful

Scale is not something that we have consciously been made aware of. We have all heard people say, "I can wear a smaller size if the garment is expensive," or "in designer clothes, I can buy a size smaller." The difference, however, is less size than scale. Let's take a look at what I mean by scale, overscale, and proper fit.

The proportion that one object bears to another is what we mean here with respect to style. The first object is you; the second is your clothing. The scale of one should be in proportion to the other.

What proportion is best? The *balanced* proportion—when your clothing looks not only as though it fits you perfectly, but also looks expensive and elegant. This right proportion also has the ability to help you look thinner if you are a little overweight and to add some weight if you are too thin.

American women seem to have a horrible obsession with wearing clothes that don't fit and buying the smallest size possible. If we can squeeze into a size six instead of our usual size eight, we must be getting thinner! Psychologically we feel good—or do we? Small looks cheap and skimpy and makes you look heavier because you can see the bulges. Or it makes you seem too thin because your bones show.

I have a friend whose attitude illustrates this passion for small sizes perfectly. She considers any garment above a size eight unacceptable. Whenever I buy a dress or jacket and share the joy of my newfound treasure with her, her response is never, "it looks wonderful on you," or "the color is beautiful," or even "how much did it cost?" Her consuming interest is always "what size is it??" Don't envy the woman who prides herself on wearing a size two; instead, emulate the woman who wears the proper size clothing for her body regardless of its numerical designation.

Learn to recognize the dividing line between elegant and too-tight or cheap. Notice that proper fit is neither overly roomy nor snug. It is simply the right proportion. Instead of being concerned about what size clothing you buy, focus on how it fits. This chart can help you determine your proper fit:

Proper Fit: for standard pieces of clothing

- **Blouse**

set-in sleeve: when you reach for shoulder bone or top of shoulder, seam should be at, or just outside of shoulder bone (not inside)

sleeve length should be at wrist bone

sleeve width: there should be at least 1½" of double fabric when you reach up and pinch the sleeve away from your upper arm

buttons must remain closed with at least 1" of fabric on each side of bustline

at midriff there should be 2" of double fabric as you reach up and pinch the fabric from each side (this will allow for proper blousing)

length of blouse should be no shorter than hipbone

- **Skirt**

pleats should never pull open; there should be no crease or pull across break of leg

pockets must remain closed and should not pull open

straight skirts should hang from buttocks in a straight line and not curve under

skirt should not ride up when you sit

hip line: there should be at least 1" of extra fabric when you pull the skirt from your body at hip line

waistband should be loose enough to allow for two fingers to be inserted

thighs must not show; you should be able to easily turn your skirt around your body

panty line must not show

Chart continues on the next page.

● **Jacket**

shoulder should be at least 1″ wider than shoulder bone

collar must not wrinkle across back

when buttoned, the coat should allow for sweater or blouse and still not pull across shoulder or hip. There should be 1½″ of extra fabric at midriff

sleeve length should allow for ½″ to ¼″ of blouse sleeve to show

sleeve width should allow for blouse or sweater, and still have ½″ of extra fabric

back: there should be no pull across back

pockets must remain closed; any pleat or dart must lie flat

● **Slacks**

pleats must remain closed

zippers and closings must lie flat

pants leg should fall straight from hip with no curve under at buttocks

pockets should not gap or pull open

hip: there must be at least 1 to 1½″ of fabric when you pull the fabric from your hip bone

waist should be big enough to allow the fingers to be inserted

panty line must not show

NOTE: Jacket, skirt, and slack lengths will be covered later.

What Does "Overscale" Mean?

Now that we have defined scale in terms of fit, let's consider the term "overscale." Some of our most famous designers create clothing that is big, loose, and roomy. This is how I define overscale, which must be considered for balance and proportion as well as for a distinctive fashion look. Who can wear overscale clothing?

Let's first consider the overscale look itself apart from the look as a fashion trend. Most of the designers who create overscale clothing design for people who are tall and thin. Since we are looking for a balance with body size, we'll visualize the person who is 5'8" tall and very thin.

She probably has very long arms and legs and looks willowy—even, at times, lanky. If you saw her in her bikini you might think of her as "all arms and legs" and a bit out of proportion. So you see, all of you people out there who are short or average in height, the tall, thin model is not so perfect after all. I have just labeled her "out of proportion." In order to make her seem *in* proportion, she needs clothes that are out of proportion—

Exaggerated shapes and lengths create a more dramatic presentation and are often necessary for balance and harmony for the very tall or large-boned person.

overscale—by normal standards. The resulting picture is one of balance and harmony. (If she wears a normally scaled outfit, a Chanel jacket or standard blazer, it will look skimpy and she will appear to overpower her clothing. She may seem too thin or too tall.) Tall women like Jane Fonda, Princess Diana, and Nancy Kissinger need the elegantly loose-fitting overscale look. They need the fuller cut to balance their height, and their long arms and legs. This overscaling must be in the body and torso of the garment as well as in the lengths of sleeves, jackets, skirts, and slacks.

I, too, am 5'8" tall, and am making progress in finding my best look. I know that I look awkward and out of proportion in clothing that is not overscale, and that I need broader shoulders, fuller sleeves, and longer torso and skirt lengths to balance my long arms and legs.

It is very difficult for the woman who is under 5'6" tall to wear clothing by designers who design for tall models. She actually looks much better in clothing that is proportioned for her scale —in skirt lengths, sleeve lengths, and body proportions that are made for her height. But even though she will look lost in an overscale article of clothing, this woman is lucky. Almost all of the moderate-priced designers and manufacturers use an average scale, and even a few of the international designers do. The woman of average height thus has many more choices. She can create expensive designer looks for far less money. Jane Pauley, Pat Nixon, and Ali MacGraw are women who wear average-scale clothing.

The woman who is short is likely to have more difficulty finding properly scaled clothing than her tall counterpart. Occasionally, however, designers and manufacturers produce clothing in size two, which is in effect scaled down. Many are now designing a special petite scale with shorter arms, skirt lengths, shoulders, and midriffs. The total body is scaled down, which is important for a balanced look.

Styles oriented to the Orient

In Japan, where 95 percent of the population is short by American and European standards, many of the women wear clothing by designers of overscale clothing. Most of them look wonderful and there is a reason for this. Designers rarely export directly to Japan. They license their designs to Japanese manufacturers who then make clothing to Japanese scale. When I first tried to buy clothes in Japan, even those by U.S. designers such as Calvin Klein, Geoffrey Beene, and Liz Claiborne were too small for me. They were scaled down for a shorter, smaller person. Perhaps we will see more designers using differing scales so that we will all have an opportunity to have a wider choice and selection in the future.

Just as leading designers favor a particular line, they also favor a particular scale. Your height will be the major deciding factor in determining the scale of your clothing. If you are 5'3" or shorter, you will have to look for a small or petite scale. If you are 5'3" to 5'6" you will need an average scale, and if you are 5'7" or taller, you will need to look for overscale designs. The individual who has exceptionally long arms and legs for her height may occasionally be able to wear a scale larger than her height would suggest.

This list groups various-priced designers and manufacturers by the scale they tend to use.

- **Overscale**

  Giorgio Armani
  Perry Ellis
  Calvin Klein
  Anne Klein II
  Tahari
  Alexander Julian
  Donna Karan

  Gianni Versace
  Perry Ellis Portfolio
  Calvin Klein Classifications
  Norma Kamali
  Willi Wear
  Pierre Cardin
  Complice
  Claude Montana
  Carol Horn

- **Average Scale**
  Chanel
  St. John
  Castleberry
  Christian Dior
  Liz Claiborne
  Yves St. Laurent
  Albert Nipon

  Adolfo
  Jaeger
  Jones of New York
  Pendleton
  Prophecy
  Mary McFadden
  Ellen Tracy
  Carol Little

- **Petite**
  Evan Picone
  Liz Claiborne
  Joannie Char
  Country Sophisticates (Pendleton)

  Albert Nipon
  Flora Kung
  Maggie London

Notice the same garment in three different scales:

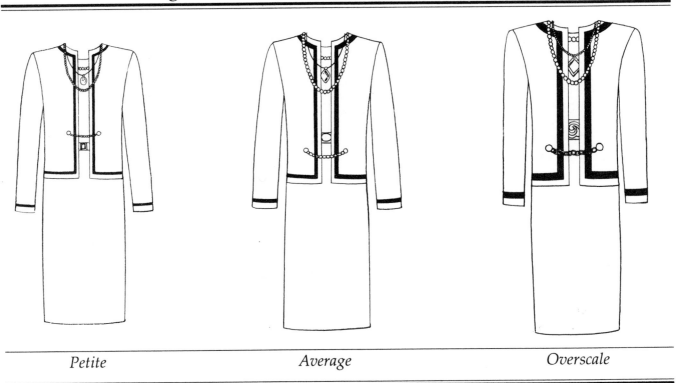

Petite   *Average*   *Overscale*

Balancing the scale

It is important to note that scale is also a vital factor in the print and design of the fabric. Those who need an overscale piece of clothing look better in prints that are large to medium in size. A small Laura Ashley print on a big overscale blouse is often out of balance. For the average-scale garment, a medium to small-sized print works well. The small scale or petite size is more balanced with a small design.

I am sure you are all familiar with the petite and vivacious lady who specializes in wearing dresses with botanical prints so large that a single stamen and petal must be continued on the back. Although she adores her large swirled prints, she would look more balanced and far more elegant in smaller proportioned prints, especially if they were also complementary to her body line. She would never make this often costly mistake if she selected her correct line and scale in her print as well as in the construction of her clothing.

The Importance of the Right Accessories

A friend of mine who has owned and managed several retail stores once told me that the first things she notices about a new customer are her shoes and handbag. She admits that the degree of salesmanship she uses with a customer is strongly influenced by not only the quality of her accessories, but their appropriateness. I'm sure she understands, without definition, the rules of my continuum line and scale proportions. How unbalanced Nancy Kissinger would look carrying a small round clutch bag. How overwhelmed Elizabeth Taylor would be by an enormous square tote.

With accessories, one has a golden opportunity to completely personalize and individualize an outfit. Have you ever been horrified by having someone show up at a particular event wearing the same dress or suit you had on? Perhaps hers looked different or even better than yours. (Some people have a real knack of adding a fabulous or even an unexpected accessory that makes the outfit stand out in the crowd.) Her secret, of course, is that she maintains the same line and scale in

A simple basic sheath can be dressed up or down with the right choice of accessories. New and creative ways of using scarves, belts and jewelry can change the overall look of an outfit from classic to romantic to an ethnic reflection of one of the themes of the season presented in the Always In Style *Portfolio.*

her accessories as she does in her clothing. She emphasizes her angles, or complements her curves. That single fabulous belt buckle, earring, or necklace in her line will often make the difference between ordinary and spectacular.

Those who need straight or sharp-straight lines in their clothing should also look for straight lines in all of their accessories. Handbags should be square or rectangular in shape and have a stiff construction. An envelope or briefcase looks fabulous when used with straight lines. A soft rounded pouch would not be consistent with straight lines of clothing and therefore would detract from the impact of an otherwise striking outfit. With soft-straight lines, either an unconstructed soft pouch or an envelope of soft leather would create a balanced look. The curved line needs a soft leather bag with small gathers, or a bag with a round or curved bottom, sides, or details.

Don't underestimate the importance of something as seemingly insignificant as a belt buckle. Square, rectangular, and geometric belt buckles are best used with straight lines. A smooth curve, oval, and shell complement a soft straight line. Circles, flowers, and swirls enhance a curved line.

Since large-size earrings are now more credible in the corporate world as well as more chic in the fashion world, it is essential that they be consistent with the lines of your face.*

*As mentioned earlier, extremes are never recommended. Contoured shapes are recommended for oval, round, heart, and pear-shaped faces. It is often advisable to select an oblong shape for the round face instead of a true circle. Similarly, a round shape will create a balance for someone with an oblong-shaped face. Straight geometric, or abstract shapes work well for those with angular face shapes. The square face may be best with rectangular and diamond shapes using the square carefully. The object is to complement your face and body line thereby enhancing your features. By choosing shapes related and not necessarily identical to your face shape you will enhance without exaggerating. The idea is to create balance and harmony.

Note the examples of proper accessories for each type.

Straight lines:

Soft-Straight lines:

Curved lines:

Varying the classic look

Everyone can wear classic pieces of jewelry such as pearls and chains. Those who need sharp-straight lines may find that baroque pearls work better than round or that a clasp that has a geometric shape will complement their facial shape better. Pearls in combination with chains or other beads also look less curved. Often a pearl earring can be set in a gold or silver geometric setting to create the right balance of size as well as line. There are many types of chains available. Some have heavy geometric links; others are finer and the links are more curved. It is always possible to combine different pieces of your jewelry to achieve the correct overall style.

Now that you've been shown how to work with your body size and shape and not against it, you will find it truly exciting to express your individuality—to enjoy being you while you are assured of looking fabulous. To help complete your perfect total look, let me end this section on line and scale with some final hints on how to cope with some of your minor flaws. Check these charts for suggestions and hints on how to enhance your individuality.

Helpful Hints For a Balanced Body

	Straight Lines	*Soft-Straight Lines*	*Curved Lines*
Broad shoulders (Note: shoulders should be 1½″ to 2″ wider than hips to allow for clothing to hang nicely)	an asset, emphasizing the angle	an asset; may want to soften slightly with V neck, raglan, or dolman sleeves. A softly curved shoulder pad will soften any edges.	if shoulders are square you can soften with raglan or dolman sleeve use curved scoop neckline where possible
Narrow shoulders	if your facial features are extremely angular, and body thin, your shoulders can be extended with large square pads, cap sleeves, or epaulettes	add shoulder pads, boat necks, horizontal detail at shoulders	add gathers in sleeves shoulder pads that are softly rounded soft draped boat necks
Large hips	straight dresses with no belt; chemise-style overblouse with straight bottom eased skirt as long as it falls straight on bottom to maintain straight line loosely fitted, dropped belt or dropped waist stitched-down pleats straight skirts and slacks that have pleats at waist and fall straight from hip use tightly woven fabric to maintain straight lines center seam or inverted pleat	eased, unpressed, gathered or gored skirt loose overblouse belts worn low easement or pleats in waist of slacks and skirts dresses that fall softly from shoulders	eased skirt flared skirt, soft pleats and gathers loose flowing top loose overblouse with slightly fitted waist

Helpful Hints For a Balanced Body (*continued*.)

	Straight Lines	*Soft-Straight Lines*	*Curved Lines*
Large bust	V necklines open collars—straight lapels long sleeves (do not stop sleeve at bustline) no breast pockets or details at bust level vertical lines	V necklines scoop necklines open collar; straight or curved lapels no breast pockets or vertical detail sleeve should not stop at bustline	scoop necklines open neck with shawl collar or curved lapels fuller bust is complementary to this line—enjoy it
Small bust	adds to the impact of the straight line horizontal lines can be added pockets and details at bustline vertical detail at bustline	works fine with this line texture, tweed, layering will add volume loose unconstructed tops so appropriate for this line are perfect pockets and details at bustline	bows, drapes, cowl necks and gathers will add curved fullness embroidery and soft details at bustline yokes are especially good for this line
Long neck	positive for this look can add high or standup collar big jewelry high necklines turtlenecks	turtlenecks high collars scarves large jewelry	scarves necklines with bows and gathers, ruffles jewelry with curved lines soft rolled high collars
Short necks	open necklines long necklaces V necks	open necklines scarves tied low V or U shaped neck	U-shaped necks open collars with bows tied low

NOTE: Never try to *change* your body line, enhance it!

Helpful Hints for Your Face Shape and Hairstyle

- **Diamond-shaped face**
  wonderful cheekbones that should be emphasized with angular hair styles
  may wish to add width across forehead with fullness or bangs

- **Square face**
  emphasize the angles by asymmetric styles, geometric cuts
  may wish to add height to create a balance with total body height by adding fullness on top to lengthen face
  off-center part or bangs are suggested

- **Rectangular face**
  emphasize angles—try asymmetric style, geometric cuts
  may wish to shorten effect with bangs and hairstyles with no fullness on top to balance body and neck lengths— an off-center part will help

- **Round face**
  emphasize curves with soft hairstyle
  may wish to add height to balance neck and body proportions—add fullness on top

- **Oblong face**
  emphasize the soft, smooth lines
  may wish to use bangs and hairstyle with no height to shorten effect—an off-center part will help

- **Pear-shaped face**
  emphasize soft curves
  may wish to add fullness across forehead with soft curls to balance narrow forehead with fuller cheeks
  hair brought onto cheeks will soften and diminish cheek width

- **Heart-shaped face**
  emphasize curves
  may use an off-center part to soften forehead and add fullness at chin level

Note: Do not try to change the line of your face; learn to enhance it!

Your individual style now has a foundation. Now that you have some guidelines and parameters to work with to enhance your physical characteristics, let's look at ways to incorporate your personality into your individual style.

The Three Faces of Fashion

What is "high" fashion? As elusive as the definition might be, there seem to be three distinct levels of fashion in the world today. High fashion can be defined as the styles that are introduced each year in Paris, Milan, and New York by the world's leading fashion designers. These designers cater to those fortunate women who have the desire and affluence to own beautifully made status clothing. The colors, fabrics, prints, and silhouettes favored by these designers are immediately copied and reinterpreted for millions of women of more limited means, who are just as interested in following current fashion trends.

The second level of fashion has more to do with the real world, where manufacturers

High fashion looks are often created by an exaggeration of scale or proportion. The unusual mix of styles and shapes also creates drama. Crisp, clean military styling combined with a casual design and soft fabrication demonstrates a paradox of styles that reflects a sophisticated look.

create clothing for the great number of women who dress for their day-to-day jobs and lifestyles. These women want to look appropriately dressed and efficient as they pursue their various careers. Their clothing styles may lean toward the classic, but they keep their fashion appeal.

There is yet another group of women: the innovators. To these women, fashion means experimenting with the new and often outrageous offerings that spark the volatile fashion scene from season to season. The innovators have the personality and drive that it takes to be first with something new and different. *Which type are you?*

I contend that high fashion is really nothing more than an exaggeration of scale, line, or detail. The recent trend toward overscale clothing is an exaggeration of scale. (Some of the exaggerated looks, such as the Comme des Garçon which came from Japan several years ago, were so exaggerated that they created a sloppy and unkempt effect. Fortunately, these looks are being replaced by a more attractive exaggerated proportion.)

How much exaggeration is appropriate? In order to avoid an extreme or trendy image and still achieve an exaggerated fashion look, it is important to exaggerate the scale by one size beyond your elegantly loose fit. This year shoulders are wider, skirt lengths are very long or very short, jackets are either long or short and worn with contrasting lengths in skirts, pants are back and are tapered, baggy, or cropped. It is important to watch the trends from season to season as designers enjoy the challenge of change.*

Who can wear the exaggerated or high-fashion looks? It all depends on who you are inside. If you have the desire, personality, and knowledge to wear the look—and wear it with confidence—you can do it. This assumes that it is appropriate for the occasion. We have covered this earlier and summarized the information in the appropriate occa-

---

*At the end of the book I will tell you how to send for your *Always in Style Portfolio*. Each season you will receive a new edition to enable you to keep abreast of the trends. The portfolio will interpret these trends for your particular body line, so that there will be no more guessing about which of the new styles will be the most complementary for you.

sions chart on page 21. You now also have the knowledge to find your right line and scale. Let's find out if you have the personality to exaggerate it!

A question of personality

Here are some simple questions relating to your personality. Please answer them honestly.

- Are you outgoing and extroverted?
  ☐Yes ☐No

- Are you the first in your town or group
  to try a new hairstyle?
  ☐Yes ☐No

- Do you love the unexpected?
  ☐Yes ☐No

- Do you enjoy being noticed?
  ☐Yes ☐No

- Are you sophisticated?   • Do you love clothes?
  ☐Yes ☐No   ☐Yes ☐No

- Are you conservative and cautious?
  ☐Yes ☐No

- Have you had the same or similar hairstyle
  for several years?
  ☐Yes ☐No

- Are you satisfied with your current wardrobe?
  ☐Yes ☐No

- Are you applying your makeup the same way
  you did five years ago?
  ☐Yes ☐No

- Do you keep your skirt length   • Are you shy or reserved?
  the same year after year?   ☐Yes ☐No
  ☐Yes ☐No

If you answered yes to the first six questions, you're ready for a high fashion look. If you answered yes to the last six, you are more conservative but still want to strive for a fashionable look. If your answers were mixed, you probably don't want to start with an extreme, but to lean in a high-fashion direction.

Remember that conservative and high fashion are not two separate looks. Instead, there is a whole spectrum from the most extreme to the most conservative, with many steps along the way. You can therefore always experiment by reaching out in a fashion direction slowly. Lengthen or shorten a skirt a little more than average, add a looser top and new belt, wear a flat shoe or a loose trouser. If it works for you and you feel comfortable, keep going. Some of you will reach further than others.

Those of you who have no desire for a high-fashion look may be comfortable with an elegantly loose fit and your proper line. That is fine, as long as you reach in the direction of the current fashion trends. You can look current and fashionable even though you are conservative. Lengthen or shorten your skirt just a little, add a new jacket, add small shoulder pads to your dress or jacket. Update your look. Those of you who want the high-fashion look will have to exaggerate more. Add a larger shoulder pad, wear skirts to your ankle or above your knee. But be sure to start with your proper fit and scale it up slowly, until you reach a maximum of one size larger than your elegantly loose fit.

As always, there are certain guidelines to consider in determining just how long or short you can wear your jackets and skirts for either a fashionably conservative or a high-fashion look and still adapt the lengths to you personally. I have already suggested scaling up your clothing by one size; now let's look at your possible lengths.

Keeping it all in proportion

We have discussed "ideal" body and facial shapes. There are also "ideal" body proportions. The ideal body is supposed to be in four equal portions, from the top of the head to the underarm; from the underarm to the break of the leg; from the break of the leg to the knee; and from the knee to the floor, as shown in this illustration.

The ideal body can be divided into four equal portions:

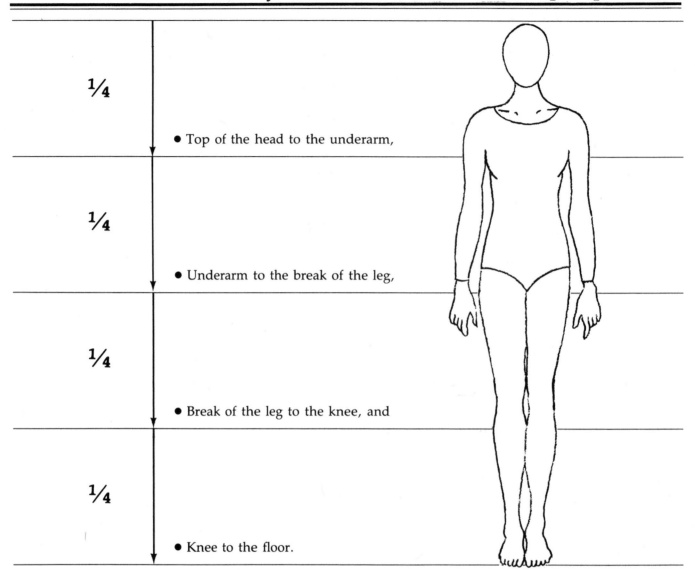

¼

● Top of the head to the underarm,

¼

● Underarm to the break of the leg,

¼

● Break of the leg to the knee, and

¼

● Knee to the floor.

You may not be equally proportioned. By understanding where you are long or short, you will learn how to best adapt any fashion to your specific needs.

For instance, you can change how long your legs look by changing your jacket length—but how much you can change it depends on your individual proportion.

Once again, if your body is not "equally" proportioned, don't worry about trying to make it seem so. You should merely understand where you are long or short so that you know how long or short you can wear your skirts and jackets as fashion trends change.

How not to look older

The first thing to do is to decide what look you are trying to achieve. We should all look fashionable and lean in the direction of the most current looks. Many people say that they want to find one length for their skirts and jackets and keep them there forever! It is, of course, more convenient, but you will also look *outdated*. Your clothes will look like the ones you wore years ago, which will make you look older. It's like putting on your makeup the same way that you did when you first started wearing it. I often tell my classes that I can tell how old you are by the way you put on your makeup: 1950's style, 1960's, or 1940's! There's no question that it's a bit inconvenient to hem your skirts periodically, but you will look so much better, so much more youthful, and like you care about yourself. The extra time and effort are well worth it. It doesn't take much to update your clothing; it is often no more than a matter of an inch in one direction or the other.

Legs: knowing where you stand

In my line and proportion class, I sketch your body and determine which quarter of your body is long and which is short. If you are long or short from your head to your underarm, it is not critical. I am more interested in your leg length, especially from your knee down, and your torso length. Look at areas A and B on this illustration.

How can these figures wear longer skirts and still flatter their legs?

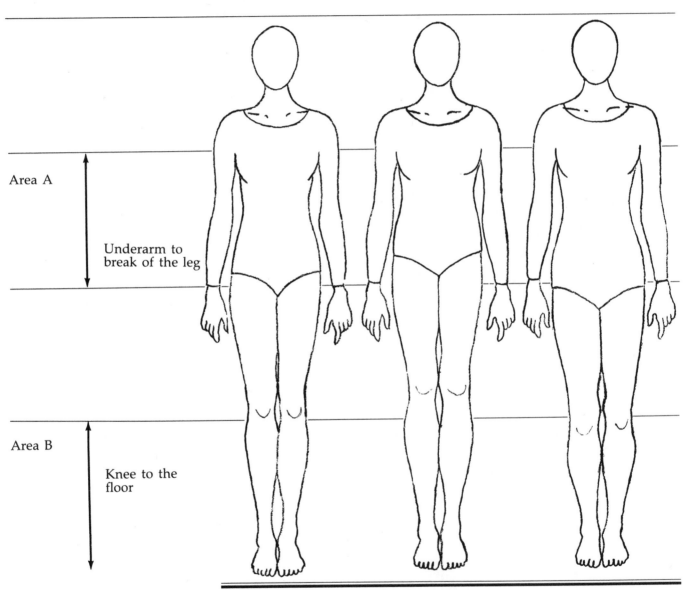

Area A

Underarm to break of the leg

Area B

Knee to the floor

Ideal Body

This figure is long from the knee to the floor.

This figure is short from the knee to the floor.

Let's look at the length from your knee to the floor. If your leg is long from the knee to the floor, you can wear your skirts very long when the styles are long and still have enough leg showing for the skirt to be flattering to your leg. If short skirts are in style, you must be careful. If you wear your skirt too short, your leg will look so long that it will seem out of proportion. You can achieve the look of a shorter skirt by wearing your skirt a little longer and lengthening your jacket. The result: your skirt will appear shorter. You have managed to achieve a fashionable look and still complement your leg.

If your leg is short from the knee down and you want to wear long skirts, you must be careful. In order to have enough of your leg showing for the skirt to be flattering to your leg, you can't make your skirt too long. You don't have enough room. However, you can shorten your jacket, which will make the skirt appear longer. You will be able to wear very short skirts when they are in style but you must be careful that your jacket does not get too long. We still want to see some skirt! It's all basically an optical illusion. By understanding where you are long and short, and understanding the fashion trends, you will know how to adjust your clothing lengths.

In the Chanel days the fashionable look was one of equal proportions. This too can be achieved by changing your skirt and jacket lengths. Use this information to create the look you want, rather than as a means of "judging" the perfection of your body. Your body and facial size and shape and your proportions are "you." Work with them to develop your own style.

Total Style

This chart summarizes your total style. Select your body line (straight, soft-straight, or curved), and go on to find your fashion direction.

Find Your Line

	Straight Lines	*Soft-Straight Lines*	*Curved Lines*
Body shapes	triangle rectangle square	rectangle ellipse	oval circle
Face shapes	diamond rectangle square	oval square oblong rectangle/softened	oval heart pear round oblong
Clothing lines	straight exterior line straight detail lines	soft-straight exterior lines straight exterior lines with soft fabric and unconstructed lines straight details on soft fabric contoured exterior lines	curved exterior lines curved details soft-straight details

FABRIC   Choose one in your line:

	Straight Lines	*Soft-Straight Lines*	*Curved Lines*
Fine fabric/ small details	☐	☐	☐
Average weight fabric/ average details	☐	☐	☐
Heavy weight fabrics/ large detail	☐	☐	☐

Chart continues on the next page.

FABRIC (*continued*)

	Straight Lines	*Soft-Straight Lines*	*Curved Lines*
Texture	little	maximum	little
Print	geometric abstract stripe sharp plaid herringbone houndstooth check	stripe paisley plaid realistic tweed	floral watercolor swirl rounded

SCALE   Choose one in your line:

	Straight Lines	*Soft-Straight Lines*	*Curved Lines*
Overscale **5'7" and over**	☐	☐	☐
Average scale **5'6" to 5'3"**	☐	☐	☐
Petite **5'3" and under**	☐	☐	☐
Accessories	geometric/angular constructed square diamond rectangle	geometric/soft unconstructed constructed with soft material oval ellipse	curved soft constructed round floral oval

Chart continues on the next page.

ACCESSORIES Choose one for your line:

	Straight Lines	Soft-Straight Lines	Curved Lines
Large accessories (overscale)	☐	☐	☐
Medium (average)	☐	☐	☐
Small/medium (petite)	☐	☐	☐

FASHION DIRECTION Choose one for your line:

	Straight Lines	Soft-Straight Lines	Curved Lines
High fashion (exaggerated scale and accessories)	☐	☐	☐
Conservative high fashion (slight exaggeration)	☐	☐	☐
Conservative fashionable (classic with fashion direction)	☐	☐	☐

Making your choice the right choice

Today's fashion designers and manufacturers offer exciting options to each of us, whatever our body type and personal style. It is no longer a matter of designers "dictating" what we should wear. You and I can choose the fashion styles that best suit our own particular body type, personality, and lifestyle. Each new season brings changes that make shopping more exciting than ever, especially when you know how to incorporate them into your own personal style of dressing.

Q. *Every season the designers give us new looks and introduce new colors. How can we follow their lead and change our wardrobes each season without spending a fortune?*

A. Fashion designers give us a *direction*. Although it's important to lean in this fashion direction to look current and fashionable, no one needs to radically change her wardrobe from season to season. You only need to take a few of the many steps that lead to the latest high-fashion look. Move slowly in the season's new direction. Even a little change will make you look youthful and up-to-date. It will also make you feel good about yourself!

Q. *I have attended a "line and design" class. I have been told the best length to wear my jackets and skirts. Does that mean I should ignore the fashion trends? I don't necessarily want a high-fashion look, but I do want to look fashionable.*

A. The ideal body can be divided vertically into four equal sections: the head to the underarm, the underarm to the break of the leg, the break of the leg to the knee, and the knee to the floor. If you want to look as though you have these ideal proportions, the lengths you were given are correct. Each year, however, different proportions are considered new and exciting. (The designers change these proportions not to be difficult but because they understand the need for change in our lives.) Because in order to grow as individuals we must constantly learn and try new things, it is important to understand how to adapt your proportions to new fashion looks. By knowing where you are long or short you can better understand how to change your jacket and skirt lengths from year to year. How much will depend on your proportions, your desires, and the fashion direction.

PART SIX

IN COLOR

Determining Your Primary and Secondary Color Palettes

Primary

Your dominant color characteristic, the one that everyone sees when they first look at you, determines your primary color palette. *Are you Deep, Light, Bright, Muted, Warm or Cool?*

1.   The easiest for most people to see are Deep, Light and Bright.

2.   Since the other colorings are in the mid-tone ranges, it is necessary to look a little further to determine the dominant characteristic of either Warm or Cool, or the more neutral Muted.

Secondary

Once you determine your primary characteristic, a secondary characteristic will also be discernible, although perhaps less obvious.

Primary with Secondary

By combining your primary and secondary palettes, you will be able to personalize your palette and have even more options.

On the facing page are illustrations of four different types of coloring. Look at the faces and read the text that I've written to show you how I decided their coloring.

Light Complexion, Blue Eyes and Blonde Hair

With blonde hair and blue eyes, the dominant characteristic projected is Light. The pastel and medium shades of the light palette will always complement this woman's light coloring. Does she have a secondary characteristic too? Sometimes personality is an important consideration. She has a level of sophistication that can carry some brighter shades and more dramatic color combinations using bright colors. Her coloring would therefore be classified as **Light/Bright**.

❏ Deep ☑ Light ☑ Bright ❏ Muted ❏ Warm ❏ Cool

Medium Complexion, Brown Eyes and Dark Hair

With dark hair and hazel/brown eyes the dominant characteristics, this coloring is Deep. Dark, rich colors worn together or with contrast are always complementary. However, her hazel eyes have a bright quality too. She can add bright clear colors. Since both her primary and secondary characteristics, Deep and Bright, are close, the ultimate decision will depend on her personal preference. Her coloring would therefore be classified as **Deep/Bright or Bright/Deep.**

☑ Deep ❏ Light ☑ Bright ❏ Muted ❏ Warm ❏ Cool

Warm & Dark Complexion, Brown Eyes and Dark Hair

With golden brown skin and honey brown eyes, the dominant characteristic of this woman is Warm. The golden colors of the warm palette will complement the green and brown in her eyes as well as her golden skintone. However, this woman has a strength and sophistication to her coloring that will be further enhanced by combining the medium warm tones with the darker rich colors of the deep palette. Her coloring would therefore be classified as **Warm/Deep**.

☑ Deep ❏ Light ❏ Bright ❏ Muted ☑ Warm ❏ Cool

Medium Complexion, Light Brown Eyes and Medium Hair

With soft ash brown hair, light brown eyes and little contrast to her coloring, the dominant characteristic of this woman is Muted. The soft blended colors of the muted palette will always look elegant on her. The neutrals, especially the cocoas and no color colors, will provide the foundation colors of her wardrobe. However, after a closer look it is clear that this woman has a golden tone to her skin. She will be able to add some of the warm colors to her muted palette, especially in selecting her makeup colors. Her coloring would therefore be classified as **Muted/Warm.**

❏ Deep ❏ Light ❏ Bright ☑ Muted ☑ Warm ❏ Cool

Deep

The Deep Palette

The Deep palette contains strong, rich colors that range from mid-tones to colors that appear almost black. They can be clear and bright or more muted. The true shades will always be complementary. However, yellow or blue undertones can be added in moderation for variety. Very light, icy colors can be used for contrast or as accents.

Deep Characteristics for All People

Caucasian
Hair: Dark: black to deep brown, chestnut, auburn; may have some warm undertones.
Eyes: Deep: brown, brown-black, hazel, rich green or olive; not blue.
Skin: Beige, olive, bronze.

African-American
Hair: Black, brown-black.
Eyes: Black, brown-black, red-brown, brown.
Skin: Blue-black, deep brown, rose-brown, mahogany, bronze.

Asian
Hair: Blue-black, black, brown-black, chestnut, dark brown.
Eyes: Black, brown-black, red-brown.
Skin: Olive, bronze, beige.

Recommended Colors

Blues: Periwinkles, royals, navies, blue-black

Greens: Blue-green, emerald, pine, turquoise, teal

Yellows: Bright lemon yellow

Oranges: Deep russets, rust

Reds: Tomato, true red, rich burgundy, magenta

Violets: Purple, aubergine, plum

Neutrals: Black, white, grays, taupes, chocolate brown

Use with Care: Monochromatic looks, medium-toned pastels such as sky blue, light green, medium yellow, orange sorbet, medium pink, lavender. Medium grays such as gray flannel.

Typical Deep Hair Colors

Typical Deep Eye Colors

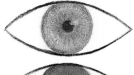  

Deep Makeup Colors

Blush	*Lipstick*	*Lip Pencil*	*Shadow*	*Eyeliner*	*Mascara*
❑ Sandlewood	❑ Plum Rose	❑ Red	❑ Champagne	❑ Sable	❑ Brown
❑ Geranium	❑ Hot Red	❑ Simply Red	❑ Peach	❑ Amethyst	❑ Black
	❑ French Brandy	❑ Sienna	❑ Taupe	❑ Gray	❑ Navy
		❑ Persimmon	❑ Purple Passion	❑ Teal	
			❑ Sea Green	❑ Brown	
			❑ Gray	❑ Taupe	

Light

The Light Palette

The Light palette contains colors ranging from soft pastels to mid-tones. They can be clear and bright or soft and muted. In the light and mid-range, colors will not appear too bright. Shades that range from a slightly warm tone to a more rosy tone will be complementary. Darker shades should be used away from the face or in combination with lighter tones.

Light Characteristics for All People

Caucasian
Hair: Most often blond: light to dark, ash or golden.
Eyes: Blue, blue-green, green, aqua; not deep hazel or brown.
Skin: Light: ivory to soft beige, pink or peach; little contrast.

African-American
Hair: Soft black, brown-black, light brown, red-brown, ash brown.
Eyes: Soft black, brown, rose-brown.
Skin: Light brown, caramel, rose-beige, cocoa.

Asian
Hair: Brown-black, ash brown, brown, soft black.
Eyes: Red-brown, brown-black, black, gray-black, golden brown.
Skin: Rose-beige, ivory, pink, peach, beige.

Recommended Colors

Blues: Baby, sky, periwinkle, soldier blue, grayed navy

Greens: Blue-greens, turquoise, aqua

Yellows: Lemon yellow, buff, chamois

Oranges: Coral, peach, coral-pink

Reds: Watermelon, strawberry, geranium, rose, pink

Violets: Lavender, violet

Neutrals: Taupe, cocoa, rose-beige, grays, soft whites

Use with Care: Strong contrast between darks and lights, black, dark navy, intense greens, dark pumpkin and rust

Typical Light Hair Colors

Typical Light Eye Colors

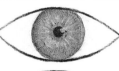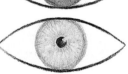
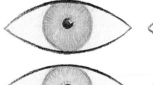

Light Makeup Colors

Blush
❏ Mango
❏ Soft Pink

Lipstick
❏ Spring Fling
❏ Antique Rose
❏ Geranium

Lip Pencil
❏ Flamingo
❏ Persimmon
❏ Pink (Rose)
❏ Melon

Shadow
❏ Champagne
❏ Peach
❏ Taupe
❏ Sea Green
❏ Smokey Blue
❏ Gray
❏ Dusty Plum

Eyeliner
❏ Taupe
❏ Gray
❏ Teal
❏ Amethyst
❏ Brown

Mascara
❏ Brown
❏ Purple
❏ Navy

Bright

The Bright Palette

The Bright palette contains bright, clear, true colors, often called the primary colors. They range from mid-tones to deeper tones that remain clear and do not appear muted or grayed down. If deep colors are used, they must be used with white or a bright color near the face. Two deep colors together will appear heavy, as will muted shades.

Bright Characteristics for All People

Caucasian
Hair: Medium to dark: brown, from ash to golden, black.
Eyes: Bright and clear: blue, blue-green, turquoise, gray, light hazel.
Skin: Light: ivory, porcelain or beige; translucent quality.

African-American
Hair: Black, brown-black, ash brown.
Eyes: Black, brown-black.
Skin: Light-medium brown, deep beige, cocoa, caramel.

Asian
Hair: Black, brown-black, dark brown.
Eyes: Black, brown-black, hazel.
Skin: Ivory, porcelain.

Recommended Colors

Blues: Periwinkle, true blue, soldier blue, clear navy

Greens: Blue-green, true green, emerald, turquoise

Yellows: Lemon yellow

Oranges: Coral-pink, coral, orange

Reds: True red, geranium, magenta, fuchsia, pink

Violets: Purple

Neutrals: Black, white, grays, taupes

Use with Care: Monochromatic looks, muddy colors, muted blues, grayed olive, bronze and brass tones, burnt oranges, brick reds, gray-beiges and muted neutrals

106

Typical Bright Hair Colors

Typical Bright Eye Colors

Bright Makeup Colors

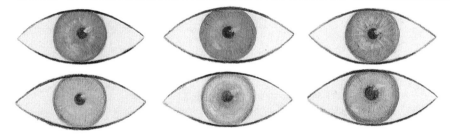

Blush
- ❏ Sandlewood
- ❏ Geranium

Lipstick
- ❏ Geranium
- ❏ Soft Pink

Lip Pencil
- ❏ Persimmon
- ❏ Flamingo
- ❏ Simply Red
- ❏ Mango

Shadow
- ❏ Champagne
- ❏ Peach
- ❏ Taupe
- ❏ Purple Passion
- ❏ Sea Green
- ❏ Gray
- ❏ Smokey Blue

Eyeliner
- ❏ Sable
- ❏ Gray
- ❏ Teal
- ❏ Brown
- ❏ Taupe

Mascara
- ❏ Brown
- ❏ Black
- ❏ Navy

Muted

The Muted Palette

The Muted palette contains soft, blended, grayed-down colors that range from mid-tones to rich, deep colors. Often even lighter shades, no color colors also work well. These colors can lean in either the warm or cooler range as long as they don't project an exaggeration of either undertone.

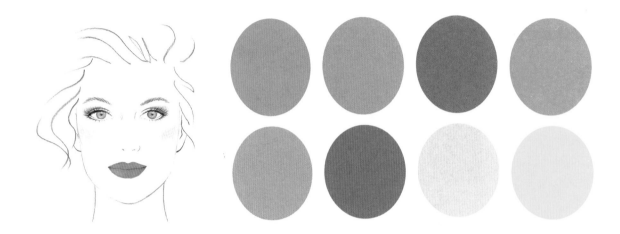

Muted Characteristics for All People

Caucasian
Hair: Medium range: medium ash brown to dark ash blond.
Eyes: Grayed green, hazel, brown-green, brown (medium to dark), green or teal.
Skin: Ivory, beige, bronze; golden freckles and ruddiness common.

African-American
Hair: Brown, ash brown, brown-black.
Eyes: Brown-black, black, gray-brown, hazel, rose-brown.
Skin: Light brown, cocoa, rose-brown, beige; opaque, freckles, absence of strong color.

Asian
Hair: Brown, mahogany, ash brown, soft black.
Eyes: Brown, rose-brown, hazel, brown-black, gray-brown.
Skin: Beige, rose-beige, bronze; absence of color; opaque, freckles.

Recommended Colors

Blues: Grayed blues, marine navy

Greens: Jade, grayed greens, olive, blue-green, teal, turquoise

Yellows: Buff, gold

Oranges: Peach, coral, rust

Reds: Tomato, rich burgundy, wine, rose, pink

Violets: Plum, aubergine, purple

Neutrals: Beige, taupe, cocoa, chocolate brown, gray

Use with Care: Florescent colors, bright and clear colors such as yacht navy, emerald green, sunny yellow, true red and violet. Strong contrasting color combinations like black and white.

Typical Muted Hair Colors

Typical Muted Eye Colors

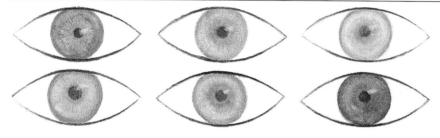

Muted Makeup Colors

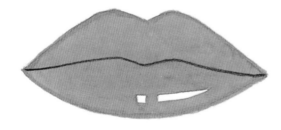

Blush
- ❏ Mango
- ❏ Sandlewood

Lipstick
- ❏ Antique Rose
- ❏ Amaretto
- ❏ French Brandy

Lip Pencil
- ❏ Melon
- ❏ Flamingo
- ❏ Sienna
- ❏ Persimmon

Shadow
- ❏ Champagne
- ❏ Peach
- ❏ Taupe
- ❏ Dusty Plum
- ❏ Moss Green
- ❏ Byzantine
- ❏ Sea Green

Eyeliner
- ❏ Brown
- ❏ Taupe
- ❏ Amethyst
- ❏ Moss
- ❏ Gray

Mascara
- ❏ Brown
- ❏ Purple
- ❏ Navy

Warm

The Warm Palette

The Warm palette contains colors with an obvious golden undertone that range from mid-tones to deeper rich tones. They can be bright and clear but often appear more muted. Some of the true colors can be added to the palette for variety, especially the greens and blues.

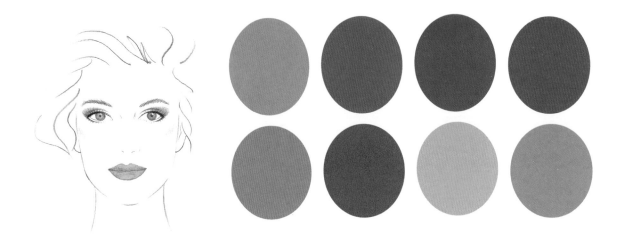

Warm Characteristics for All People

Caucasian
Hair: Medium range: blond or brown with gold, red or strawberry highlights.
Eyes: Warm: green, hazel, brown, topaz, blue-green, teal.
Skin: Golden: beige, ivory, bronze; may have freckles.

African-American
Hair: Brown, golden brown, brown-black, chestnut.
Eyes: Warm brown, topaz, deep brown, hazel.
Skin: Bronze, caramel, mahogany, golden brown, light brown, brown; freckles.

Asian
Hair: Golden brown, auburn, dark brown, chestnut.
Eyes: Warm brown, brown-black, hazel, deep brown, topaz.
Skin: Golden beige, ivory, bronze; freckles.

Recommended Colors

Blues: Periwinkle, marine navy

Greens: Olives, jade, moss, grayed greens, tobacco, turquoise, teal

Yellows: buff, chamois, gold

Oranges: Pumpkin, peach, apricot, rust, coral

Reds: Orange-red, tomato, brick

Violets: Purple, aubergine

Neutrals: Khaki, beige, camel, tan, brown, warm grays

Use with Care: Sky blue, emerald green, watermelon red, pink and blue gray.

Typical Warm Hair Colors

Typical Warm Eye Colors

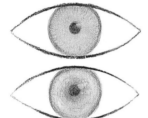 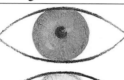 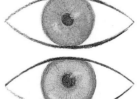

Warm Makeup Colors

Blush	*Lipstick*	*Lip Pencil*	*Shadow*	*Eyeliner*	*Mascara*
❏ Mango	❏ Apricotta	❏ Rust	❏ Champagne	❏ Brown	❏ Brown
❏ Nutmeg	❏ Amaretto	❏ Sienna	❏ Peach	❏ Taupe	❏ Black
	❏ Warm Honey	❏ Melon	❏ Brown	❏ Amethyst	❏ Purple
		❏ Flamingo	❏ Dusty Plum	❏ Moss	
			❏ Moss Green	❏ Brown	
			❏ Byzantine		
			❏ Sea Green		

Cool

The Cool Palette

The Cool palette contains colors that have blue undertones and range from mid-tone to deep shades. The true colors are often complementary additions to this palette. Colors with obvious warm undertones should be used in combination with cool colors and away from the face.

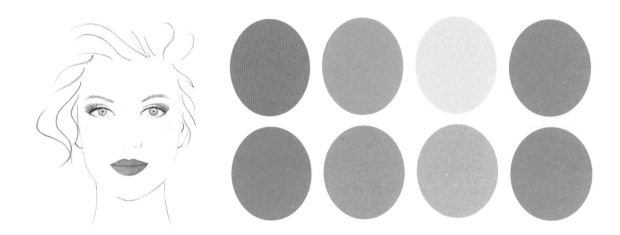

Cool Characteristics for All People

Caucasian
Hair: Ash brown (dark to medium), silver or salt and pepper.
Eyes: Cool: rose-brown, gray-brown, gray-blue.
Skin: Cool: beige, rose-beige, pink.

African-American
Hair: Black, ash brown, blue-black.
Eyes: Brown-black, black, gray-brown, rose-brown.
Skin: Rose-brown, gray-brown, cocoa, dark brown, soft blue-black.

Asian
Hair: Black, blue-black, brown-black, ash brown, dark brown, salt and pepper.
Eyes: Black, gray-brown, rose-brown.
Skin: Pink, rose-beige, gray-beige; sometimes sallow.

Recommended Colors

Blues: Periwinkles, royal, true blue, navy

Greens: Blue-greens, emerald

Yellows: Lemon yellow only as an accent

Oranges: Avoid all

Reds: Blue-reds, burgundy, wine, true red, magenta, rose, pink

Violets: Purples, plums

Neutrals: Grays, black, white, taupe, silvery khaki

Use with Care: Teal, yellow green, gold, all oranges, warm reds, golden beige, camel, most browns except one that is very pink.

Typical Cool Hair Colors

Typical Cool Eye Colors

Cool Makeup Colors

Blush
❏ Geranium
❏ Soft Pink

Lipstick
❏ Plum Rose
❏ Antique Rose
❏ Geranium

Lip Pencil
❏ Simply Red
❏ Red (Rose)
❏ Persimmon
❏ Melon

Shadow
❏ Champagne
❏ Pink Peach
❏ Taupe
❏ Purple Passion
❏ Smokey Blue
❏ Gray

Eyeliner
❏ Sable
❏ Gray
❏ Amethyst
❏ Navy
❏ Brown
❏ Taupe

Mascara
❏ Brown
❏ Black
❏ Navy

Personal Profile
Questionnaire

Dear friend:

On the following pages you will find a version of the *Always In Style Personal Profile® Questionnaire* very much like the one you will find on www.alwaysinstyle.com. You can subscribe to our service for small yearly fee or go on as an Invited Guest free of charge by clicking on the Invited Guest link. By entering the information about yourself on similar on line profiles you will receive your analysis and product recommendations selected especially for you. You will also receive monthly emails on the latest beauty and fashion trends.

1. Personal Information

NAME _____
          LAST   FIRST   MIDDLE INITIAL

ADDRESS _____

_____

STATE _____ ZIP _____

TELEPHONE: (H) (_____) _____

               (W) (_____) _____

Workplace
- ❏ I am a full-time homemaker.
- ❏ I am a full-time homemaker now, but will begin working in the near future.
- ❏ I have a full- or part-time job I do at home.
- ❏ I have a full-time job outside of the home.
- ❏ I have a part-time job outside of the home.
- ❏ I have always worked but am now retired.

What do you wear at work?
- ❏ Slacks and casual clothes
- ❏ Suits, dresses & formal styles
- ❏ A uniform

Makeup
- ❏ I wear makeup every day.
- ❏ I wear it several times a week.
- ❏ I wear it rarely.
- ❏ I never wear makeup.

Fragrance
- ❏ I wear fragrance every day.
- ❏ I wear it several times a week.
- ❏ I wear it rarely.
- ❏ I never wear it.

Occupation
- ❏ Homemaker
- ❏ Manufacturing, warehouse
- ❏ Construction, building trades
- ❏ Security, police officer
- ❏ Housekeeper, maintenance
- ❏ Agricultural worker, farmer
- ❏ Hotel, restaurant, food service
- ❏ Travel, transportation employee
- ❏ Retail sales, merchandiser
- ❏ Teacher, librarian, principal
- ❏ Doctor, nurse, health technician
- ❏ Lawyer or accountant
- ❏ Manager, administrator
- ❏ Secretary, clerical worker
- ❏ Artist, writer, designer
- ❏ Member of the Armed Forces

- ❏ Other: _____

Accessories
Check all that apply:
- ❏ I never wear jewelry or accessories.
- ❏ I wear only a ring and perhaps some simple earrings.
- ❏ I sometimes wear fashion jewelry and accessories.
- ❏ I wear jewelry and fashion accessories everyday.
- ❏ I only wear precious metals and real gemstones.

2. Age & Where You Live
- ❏ I am 25 or under
- ❏ I am 26 - 33
- ❏ I am 34 - 40
- ❏ I am 41- 50
- ❏ I am 51 - 65
- ❏ I am over 65

- ❏ I live in the country
- ❏ I live in a suburban area
- ❏ I live in a small town
- ❏ I live in a city

3. Clothing Needs
Rate your clothing needs or interests.
greatest = 1,   middle =2,   lowest = 3

	1	2	3
CASUAL	❏ 1	❏ 2	❏ 3
CAREER/OFFICE	❏ 1	❏ 2	❏ 3
DRESSY/SPECIAL OCCASION	❏ 1	❏ 2	❏ 3

4. Hair

An individual's hair color is often a combination of many colors. Check the one choice below that best describes your hair color as it is today.

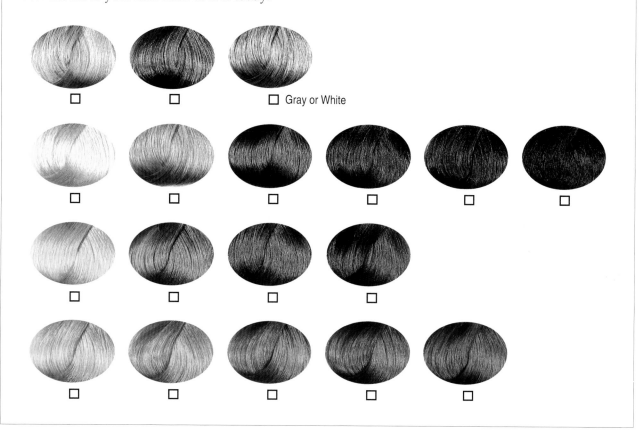

☐   ☐   ☐ Gray or White

☐   ☐   ☐   ☐   ☐   ☐

☐   ☐   ☐   ☐

☐   ☐   ☐   ☐   ☐

5. Skin tone

Check your skin tone:

Depth:	☐ Light	☐ Medium	☐ Dark
Undertone:	☐ Golden	☐ Rose	☐ Neutral
Freckles:	☐ Yes	☐ No	

What is your background?
☐ Asian
☐ African-American
☐ Hispanic
☐ Pacific Islander
☐ Native American
☐ Caucasian

☐ Other: _____

6. Lipstick

Pick your favorite lipstick color(s)

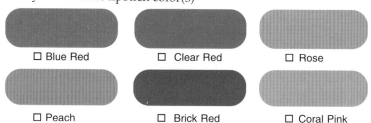

☐ Blue Red   ☐ Clear Red   ☐ Rose

☐ Peach   ☐ Brick Red   ☐ Coral Pink

In general, I prefer the following types of lipstick colors:
☐ Bright shades   ☐ Soft shades

7. Fashion Direction

Which category
best describes you?

☐ **Conservative** -
quiet colors and styles.

☐ **Contemporary Classic** -
conservative with a
fashion-forward look.

☐ **Fashion Forward** - dare to be
different and exaggerated details.

8. Eyes

An individual's eyes are often a combination of many colors.
Check the one(s) that best describes your eye color.

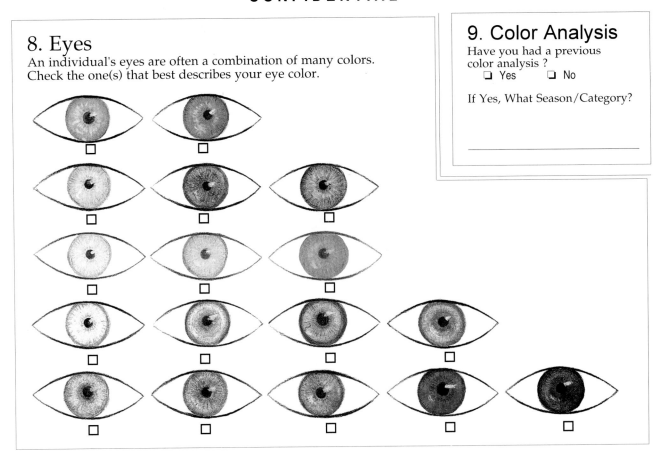

9. Color Analysis

Have you had a previous
color analysis ?
❑ Yes   ❑ No

If Yes, What Season/Category?

10. Favorite Colors

Check the color category(s) you like the most or feel the most comfortable wearing:

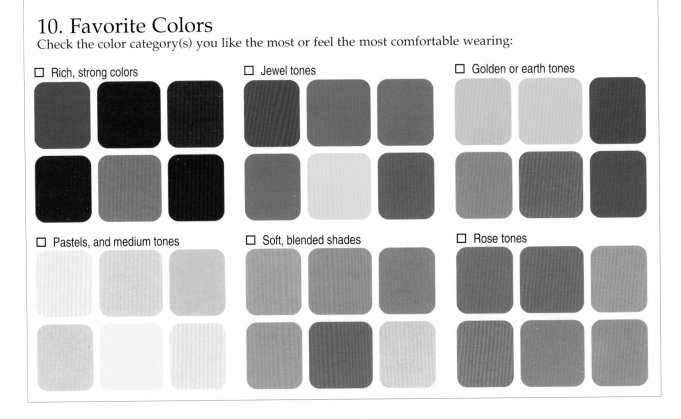

☐ Rich, strong colors

☐ Jewel tones

☐ Golden or earth tones

☐ Pastels, and medium tones

☐ Soft, blended shades

☐ Rose tones

11. Personal Statistics

Accurate measurements assist in a correct analysis.

Height = _____ feet _____ inches

Weight = _____ pounds

Bust = _____ inches
(measure across the center back through the largest portion of the bust)

Rib Cage = _____ inches
(measure around the center of the rib cage)

Waist = _____ inches
(measure around the natural waistline, keep tape loose)

Hips = _____ inches
(measure 7" below the waist)

Pant size = _____

Dress size = _____

Blouse size = _____

Check one: ☐ I have a visible waist
☐ I have little or no visible waist

12. Face Shape

Your face shape may be a combination of several shapes. Check the one(s) that best describes your face shape.

MORE ANGULAR

☐ Square
Square jaw
Straight sides

☐ Rectangle
Long face
Square jawline

☐ Diamond
Prominent cheekbones
Narrow forehead
Pointed chin

☐ Triangle
Narrow chin
Prominent cheekbones
Broad forehead

MORE CURVED

☐ Round
Soft jawline, Soft cheeks

☐ Oval

☐ Heart
Wide forehead

☐ Pear
Soft shape

13. Figure Concerns

Please indicate if you would like helpful suggestions on any of the following:

☐ long neck   ☐ short neck
☐ broad shoulders   ☐ narrow shoulders
☐ large bust   ☐ small bust
☐ long waist   ☐ short waist
☐ long legs   ☐ short legs
☐ large hips

☐ Petite (small boned, 5'2" and under)
☐ Tall (5'9" and over)

☐ I am **Plus Size** and would prefer the Full-Figure Edition of the *Personal Profile*.

For Office Use Only

PC   ☐ D ☐ L ☐ B ☐ M ☐ W ☐ C

SC   ☐ D ☐ L ☐ B ☐ M ☐ W ☐ C

PBL   ☐ S ☐ S1 ☐ S2 ☐ C

SBLL ☐ S ☐ S1 ☐ S2 ☐ C

Go to www.alwaysinstyle.com for personal advice on color, bodyline, style, skincare, hair, aromatherapy and fragrance.

For questions and additional information email us at customerservice@alwaysinstyle.com

117

PART VII
ABOUT COLOR

The Power of Color

Do you dream in black and white or in color? If you dream in color, do you remember your first technicolor dream? Mine occurred when I was seven years old—and I vividly remember it being the flower garden behind my house. Perhaps I remember because I was precocious about color, but it's more likely that I remember because that dream was so beautiful.

We were the first family on the block to have a color television set. So many friends began to "stop in" to watch TV at our house that I toyed with the idea that their visits were a tribute to my popularity. The truth, of course, was that watching television in living color was a hundred times more fun than watching in black and white.

Motion pictures fascinated the public from their earliest beginnings in grainy black and white. But their success skyrocketed with the single new introduction of color. Why was there such a disproportionate increase in these industries when they switched from black and white to color? They literally "came alive"

The impact of the outfit changes with the color. Picture how different this would look in black and white, red and black, camel and beige or pink and white.

with color, because color has both a dimensional and an emotional affect on each of us. The performers, who had been little more than remote images on our screens in black and white, became real people in color.

Colors have a profound effect on us. As Leatrice Eiseman explains in her book, *Alive With Color* (Acropolis 1983), "Colors evoke emotions—some pleasant, some very unpleasant. You can turn off to a terrific color because of some experience long past." In fact, psychological "color tests" are often given to people who are emotionally disturbed or depressed. Because we have little reason to falsify our responses to color, the technique opens up channels for investigating the problems of those who are unwilling or unable to communicate on a verbal level. Think back to what I said earlier about non-verbal communication; it will help you to recognize that color has its own special prominence, and impact.

If you were to be offered a choice between dressing in the right style or dressing in the right color, which would you choose? Style does have greater importance. But you must understand the *symbiotic effect* of using the best style *and* the best color. Each contributes to your good image, but *together, they more than double the benefits.*

You've analyzed your body type to determine what style of clothing will be best for you. You've gone beyond the visual analysis to incorporate your personality traits, adding another dimension to your wardrobe. The final dimension is that often underestimated but so crucial aspect, color. It's now time to analyze your individual coloring in order to determine your best colors—to add the final dimension to your style.

Why was Carole Jackson's book *Color Me Beautiful* such a runaway success? As I noted earlier, color has a profound psychological affect on all of us. And each of us has that wonderfully human trait called "vanity," which ensures a natural curiosity about which colors are best on us. Finally, *Color Me Beautiful* gave us simple rules about color; about its nature and use as it applies to our unique individual coloring. When introducing any new subject to millions of people, it is important to do so in a simple and logical way so that a strong foundation can be built. When we are first taught math, we are told that it is impossible to subtract five from three. Later, after the negative numbers have been introduced, we are told that we can take five from three and get negative two. This does not mean that the initial information was wrong. It merely indicates the need to continue to build and expand our knowledge to assure success and satisfaction in the future. So let's take the initial information we have received about color, expand upon it, and incorporate your personality so that you will be able to use color to imprint your own vivid individual style.

Q. *I have been in the fashion business for years. I have a natural flair for color and style. Are color and style "rules" really necessary?*

A. Your natural abilities make you one of the lucky ones. Most of us aren't so fortunate. For us, it is important to understand what to look for when selecting clothes so that we can achieve balance and harmony. But even people who have this natural ability find it fun and exciting to understand why what they have been doing works. I bet there are still times when you select something that's not quite right. By understanding the rules, you will be able to "fine-tune" your eye.

Color
Characteristics

Before we look at color and how it relates to you personally, it is important to discuss the characteristics of color. We can then form a basis of comparison between colors to see how they relate to each other and to understand how to use them most effectively. Colors are often divided into different groups as a means to study their characteristics.

Warm and Cool

One of the most common ways is to separate colors by their "basetones." Consider an orange-red and a blue-red. The orange-red has a yellow base, the blue-red a blue base. A great many colors are combinations of undertones with almost equal amounts of yellow and blue. These are called true colors. Consider an orange-red, a true red and a blue-red. In the continuum from an easily definable cool color to an obviously warm color, many colors fall in the center band. Depending on the surrounding colors, the individual's color eye and the light source, these colors can be analyzed as to whether they are primarily warm or cool and a technical decision can then be made. For our purposes, image, fashion and wearing the most complementary colors, it is best to acknowledge the fact that some colors can be called cool, some can be called warm and others are simply in between.

Depth

The second characteristic of colors is "depth" how dark or light a particular color may be. Consider a color from its darkest shade to its lightest from black to white with various shades of gray in between.

A deep red, for example, runs the gamut from dark maroon to pale pink. The steps in between represent the level of depth. We will consider both deep and light colors deep ranging from dark to medium and light from medium to pale. Obviously there are colors in the medium range that require a judgment call as to whether light or dark predominates. This is also the case with the true colors when undertones are being considered.

Brightness

Another important characteristic is "brightness." This term defines how vivid or muted a color may be. Muted or neutralized colors have been softened by adding gray or other colors to dull their intensity. Softening a brilliant fuchsia to a dusty pink is an example of how colors are toned downed or muted. Our third color characteristic considers muted and bright as definitions of clarity or intensity.

Personal Coloring

Your personal coloring has the same three characteristics undertone or basetone, depth, and level of brightness and is determined by your skintone, hair and the color of your eyes. Just as the cut of your clothes should complement your body lines, the colors you wear should enhance the colors that are really you.

The Beginning of the AIS System

After analyzing thousands of people all over the world and speaking with researchers in cosmetics labs, dermatologists, ophthalmologists, skin and hair experts and color company specialists, I realized that, like everything else in this world, determining individual color characteristics is not a black or white issue there is a big gray area.

Skintone is made up of melanin, carotene and hemoglobin. Melanin is brown to orange-red, a warm color. Carotin is clear to orange; hemoglobin is red. Only areas in the skin that are white (vitiligo) contain no melanin. Everyone's skin has some warm color, but how much? Some skin has a great deal and is easily described as golden or warm. Others have very little warm color and may even have a gray or bluish overtone that can certainly be described as cool. The great majority of people, however, have both warm and cool elements and best wear colors that are neither too cool or too warm.

Is There a Season for You?

For years color consultants argued among themselves over whether a client was Spring or Summer, Winter or Autumn. Many an analysis was missed and confusion resulted. Some of you may have had difficulty trying to decide which season best described your coloring. You may have recognized some of your characteristics in two of the seasons, each one seeming to describe your coloring.

In my first color analysis, it was determined that I was a Spring. For the first year, I wore many of the Spring colors and loved them, but found that I was not comfortable in the brightest colors of the palette. During my training to become a consultant, it was decided that I actually looked better in the colors of the Autumn palette. I knew that my first analysis was not totally wrong, since I still loved and felt good in some of the Spring colors. However, I did prefer the deeper, richer warm tones of the Autumn palette. As I looked at the skintone, hair and eye color charts, I noticed that my hair was more Spring-like, my eyes were more Autumn-like and my skintone was described in both. I saw a little of myself in both. I also knew that I really preferred neutral colors no color colors. I like muted and grayed-down shades but with a warm cast.

I realized that if I could use colors from more than one palette successfully, everyone else could do the same. I also understood the importance of being able to wear colors that are comfortable and reflect my personality. I was determined to find a way to identify more individual palettes palettes that reflected and complemented the total person.

So, is there a season for each person? Perhaps. Perhaps not. There are skintones that appear to the human eye to be neutral, neither really golden nor really pink or cool. Identifying a skintone may depend on the lighting, surrounding colors and by the fact that skintone, hair and eye colors may have both warm and cool elements. It therefore is important to determine a system that describes individual color characteristics more accurately than the seasonal color system.

An Easier and More Accurate Notation

More and more people began to accept the fact that grouping people into four color groups was a bit simplistic. Adding colors from a second palette was a start to a more accurate and expanded system. As time went on, new information was collected. What we knew about color expanded. We at Always In Style have continued to refine our system. We have discovered that the easiest, most logical and most scientific approach is to look at the characteristics of your coloring and find the one that is most obvious and best describes you.

Are you Warm or Cool?
Deep or Light? Muted or Bright?

Once your most dominant, your primary, characteristic is identified, you can then add colors from a secondary group that may better reflect your personal preferences and give you the uniqueness and flexibility you should have.

Listed below are descriptions of the primary characteristics. Find the one that best describes your coloring. You may find two. One will be your primary and one your secondary. If you do not see one that is dominant, choose the one you are most comfortable with as your primary palette.

Warm

The "warm" person projects a total golden glow. You have true golden undertones in your hair, eyes and skintone. Your hair is red, auburn, golden blonde, yellow-brown or strawberry. You may in fact have been called a redhead at some point. Your eye color is hazel, green, teal, brown or topaz. A ruddy earthtone with gold or green combinations is projected in your eye color. Your skintone is bronze, golden beige or ivory, and you often have freckles. In general, your warm coloring is medium in depth, neither very light nor very dark.

If you can describe your coloring as "warm," you will always be successful wearing warm-based colors of medium depth. You can add lighter or darker colors depending on your personality, the time of year and the occasion.

Cool

A "cool" person often has a rose or pink complexion. It is often described as soft or dusty. (Don't confuse this with peach coloring or a high red color.) Cool coloring in general is in the mid-tone range, not really dark or light.

Your hair color is ash brown, dark brown or deep ash blonde. Your hair may have some warm highlights, but they are not obvious or easily seen. Overall, it projects an ash color. Remember, everyone's hair has some red highlights. In the cool person these are subtle. As our hair grays, it loses pigment and becomes more ash-colored. Our appearance softens.

Your skintone is beige, rose-beige, pink, taupe and often projects a blue or gray undertone. Your eye color will be blue-gray, gray-blue or cool green. If brown, it is rosy or gray-brown.

If your coloring is best described as cool, you can successfully wear cool-based colors that are neither too dark nor too light. Although the cool colors will be complementary, especially as your hair grays, adding some true or warm colors as accents will lend a sophistication and elegance to your outfits.

Deep

The "deep" characteristic is the easiest to see. Do you have dark hair and eyes? If so, you're deep. How deep? Your hair color will range from black to deep brown, from a chestnut or auburn color to blue-black. Your eyes are also deep dark brown, brown-black, deep hazel or dark olive.

Although your skintone is generally a beige, it may be olive or bronze. There are both warm and cool undertones in your skintone. If you are deep you can successfully wear deep colors that are not too blue or too gold. Contrast also works well and can be achieved by adding some light accents.

Light

If your coloring can be described as "light," your hair is blonde golden or ash, medium to light. Your hair may darken when not exposed to sunlight and then rapidly lighten when bleached by the sun. Your skintone is medium to light and may appear peach or rosy. There is little contrast between your hair color and your skintone. Your eye color is gray, blue, green or a combination. Your eyes appear to change colors, from blue to gray to green. They are not brown, deep hazel or deep blue.

If you are light, you can successfully wear colors that are medium to light in depth, neither too warm nor too cool, too bright or too muted. If you are light and have a more dramatic or sophisticated personality or lifestyle, some bright colors can be added to your palette.

Bright

The "bright" person has a crisp, clear look derived from a strong contrast between skin and hair color and the jewel-like clarity of the eye color. Two types of coloring can be called bright.

The first is the person whose hair color contrasts sharply with the skintone. Your hair color is brown, sometimes even black or ash brown. Your skin color is almost transparent ivory or porcelain. Accompanying this contrast in skin and hair color: bright, clear eye color in jewel tones blue, green, turquoise or violet. They are not brown. This type of bright person has often been confused with the "deep." The brightness of the eyes alone demands a balance of clarity that is lost with colors that are too deep.

The second type of bright coloring, which has less contrast in hair and skintone, includes those whose eye color is true and jewel-like, blue, green, turquoise, etc. Your skintone is a bit more golden and your hair not as deep; eyebrows and lashes will be dark. If your coloring can be described as bright, you can successfully wear colors that are clear primary colors. When wearing dark colors, be sure to create contrast. Two deep colors worn together can be too heavy.

Muted

Muted coloring has strength, but not necessarily depth. Your hair color is light, ash blonde, ash brown or medium blonde. Your skintone ranges from golden to beige to ivory, often with an absence of any cheek color. With your light hair, your eyes may be brown, hazel or teal. The main difference between those of you who are muted and those of you who are light is in your eye color, which adds a richness and weight to your coloring. The color range is not light or dark, but medium in depth. There will be a balance that results in a kind of "no color" look. If your coloring can be described as muted, you will successfully wear softened colors of medium intensity. The neutrals used by many international designers are ideal for your muted coloring.

Choosing a Secondary Characteristic

Although we all have a primary characteristic the one that I see first when I look at you we all have a secondary and tertiary characteristic as well. Since all colors have three characteristics, an undertone, depth and clarity, so do we. The secondary and tertiary may not be as obvious or may present themselves to the human eye in equal proportions. Therefore, choosing a secondary is often a matter of personal preference since we all project a combination of our external physical and our internal self.

Let's therefore consider your secondary characteristic as a means of expanding your color choices to create your own unique and personal palette.

Personal Choices for: Deeps

If your primary characteristic is Deep, your secondary choices are Muted, Bright, Cool or Warm. Choose the secondary palette that best describes your coloring or with which you are most comfortable.

DEEP/WARM

There are Deeps who have subtle golden or red highlights in their hair. They may also notice some freckles or some bronze or golden tones in their skintone, especially with a tan. Many people who have dark hair and eyes simply like the rich, warm colors. These burnished tones are often considered sophisticated and are identified with European women. Adding the warm tones to the Deep palette and maintaining contrast will create a very elegant palette.

DEEP/BRIGHT

Many Deep people have very light complexions and/or a hazel/brown eye. These individuals look equally well in the bright clear colors as in the deep. In this case the primary and secondary characteristics are very close. Many Deep people are naturally drawn to bright colors and especially enjoy them in the warmer weather or for more casual wear.

DEEP/MUTED

Some Deeps have a neutral tone to their skin. Their brown hair and eyes are not very dark, but more ash and medium in depth, creating a softer look. Less contrast and a more monochromatic use of the deep colors is complementary. In addition, these people often like the "neutrals" or no color colors used so frequently by designers like Calvin Klein and Georgio Armani.

DEEP/COOL

As the Deep person ages and gray appears, she is often better off adding some of the cooler blue and gray tones as basics. This does not mean that the palette must be all cool. A mixture of warm and cool colors is always the most appealing. There are also some Deeps, especially those from India, Indonesia and some African countries, who have very cool or ash tones in the skintone but still demand the strong, deep colors as a primary palette for balance and harmony.

Personal Choices for: Lights

If your primary characteristic is Light, your secondary choices are Bright, Warm, Cool or Muted. Choose the secondary palette that best describes your coloring or with which you are most comfortable.

LIGHT/BRIGHT

Some Lights have hair that is between blonde and brown. Their coloring isn't strong enough to be considered Bright, but it is strong enough to add some of the bright colors. Other Lights have truly light coloring but have a more sophisticated or dramatic personality and find the light pastel colors too soft. They want or need the brighter colors to complement their overall presentation.

LIGHT/WARM

Many Lights will notice warm or golden highlights in their blonde hair. Their skintone often appears rosy but actually has a peach tone. Some lights often see a golden tone or some freckles after they have been in the sun. Adding some light warm tones like coral, peach, turquoise, buff and some of the tans and beiges will add richness and a new dimension to the light pastel palette.

LIGHT/MUTED

The pastel colors of the light palette are sometimes too delicate for the Light person with blue-green eyes and deeper blonde hair. Although she has a softness to her coloring, she needs some richer and often more sophisticated colors. The brights become overpowering either because of her more conservative personality or because of the softness in the eye color. The sage greens, teals and plums add a subtle richness. Cocoas, coffee browns and taupes are the most important in this expanded palette.

Light/Cool

A very light ash blonde or brown hair color with a softened eye color is often complemented by adding the cool rose and pink tones that many women prefer. As Lights gray, their skintone also looses some color and appears more cool. While adding some cool colors will be complementary, an effort should be made to continue to use the coral-pinks, turquoises and beiges. They will add color to the face, creating a more youthful look.

Personal Choices for: Brights

If your primary characteristic is Light, your secondary choices are Deep, Light, Warm or Cool. Choose the secondary palette that best describes your coloring or with which you are most comfortable.

Bright/Deep

Many Brights who have hazel or blue-green eyes like the richness of the deep palette and look especially well in the teals, greens and dark browns. Because they have some depth to their eye color and often have a less delicate skintone, more beige than porcelain, they can successfully add the deep colors. They often find the deep colors especially useful in the cooler weather.

Bright/Light

A true Bright whose hair is brown instead of dark brown or black is often more comfortable with some softer shades. It may be a matter of personality and the need for less dramatic colors. Some of the light colors can be added as accents and also used for shirts, blouses and lingerie, creating a softer look, especially in the summer. Care should be taken not to resort to all pastels, especially as the Bright ages. She still needs clear colors to enhance her vibrant eye color.

Bright/Warm

The Bright with flaming red hair, bright blue eyes and porcelain or freckled skin has almost equal bright and warm characteristics. Because her eyes are not warm, her primary characteristic is still Bright. However, the warmer bright shades of coral-pink, turquoise and orange-red are wonderful options. Often a brunette has auburn highlights in her hair and an ivory complexion combined with her bright eyes. She too can add some warm colors to her bright palette.

BRIGHT/COOL

Brights whose hair begins to gray or who have snow white hair often maintain the clarity and brightness of their eye color. They can certainly add some of the cool colors, especially the blues and grays. The pinks and roses provide a little softness without becoming too drab. There are brights whose hair is still dark and who need the bright clear colors but prefer the pinks and roses of the cool palette. Adding these while maintaining contrast will still provide a degree of clarity and allow for some creativity.

Personal Choices for: Warms

If your primary characteristic is Warm, your secondary choices are Bright, Light, Deep or Muted. Choose the secondary palette that best describes your coloring or with which you are most comfortable.

WARM/BRIGHT

The true Warm person has warm hair, eyes and skintone. Warms who have bright green, blue or turquoise eyes and deep red, auburn or warm brown hair will find that adding the bright colors truly enhances their coloring and beautifully expands their palette. The knowledge that the bright clear colors are especially complementary to the eye color will provide a direction for selecting warm colors that are not too heavy or muted.

WARM/DEEP

The redhead with dark brown or hazel eyes that appear almost moss green can benefit from adding colors from the deep palette. They provide the strength and contrast that create the balance and harmony for a truly personalized palette. The deep reds, emerald greens, blacks and charcoal grays offer additional complementary color choices that combine beautifully with more medium-toned warm shades.

WARM/LIGHT
Warms with light strawberry blonde hair and blue-green or turquoise eyes often like the soft pastel shades of the light palette, especially the blues and greens. The neutrals, grays and navies provide more serious career color choices than the camels and beiges of the warmer palettes and combine nicely with the corals and warm red tones. Some of the pinks from the light palette can be especially flattering and useful, especially in the warmer weather.

WARM/MUTED
Some warms have only subtle golden highlights in their hair, a soft eye color and a more neutral skintone. More important, they do not like the warm colors and find the neutrals of the muted palette more comfortable and sophisticated. Both the warm and muted palettes tend to be in the medium range, but the muted palette appears less intense, providing an opportunity for monochromatic use of colors.

Personal Choices for: Muteds

If your primary characteristic is Muted, your secondary choices are Deep, Light, Warm or Cool. Choose the secondary palette that best describes your coloring or with which you are most comfortable.

MUTED/DEEP
Although muted coloring is by nature neutral with a soft quality, those with medium brown hair and eyes and a stronger personality often like the stronger deep colors. The dark browns, greens and grays add strength to the palette, combine nicely with the muted colors and provide more options for monochromatic combinations. These deep colors are often necessary additions for a more powerful corporate look.

MUTED/LIGHT

The Muted person with blonde hair and soft hazel eyes often prefers the light pastel shades and enjoys adding some extra pinks, corals and blues to her muted palette. The combination creates a gentle, delicate look that is often considered more innocent and naive. Although perhaps not wanted at all times, on occasion this look is desirable.

MUTED/WARM

Some Muted people with ash blonde or brown hair and hazel eyes often have a very golden skintone. Others will notice some subtle golden highlights in their hair, especially in the sun. By adding some warm colors, a golden glow is often achieved. This person will often find that the warmer lipsticks and blushes are especially complementary. The warmer colors also offer some more colorful options for summer or casual wear since they often appear more informal.

MUTED/COOL

When a Muted person grays, her skintone and eye color also soften, creating a cooler look. Warm undertones that may have been visible, no matter how subtle, disappear. Although a coolness is projected and the blues, pinks, roses and grays will be flattering, care should be taken not to depend too heavily on the deeper burgundy and fuchsia tones.

Personal Choices for: Cools

If your primary characteristic is Cool, your secondary choices are Deep, Light, Bright or Muted. Choose the secondary palette that best describes your coloring or with which you are most comfortable.

COOL/DEEP

Some Cools have ash brown or gray hair and a cool or pink tone to their skintone. Yet they still project a depth, especially with their brown eyes, that is complemented by adding some of the rich tones of the deep palette. While the deeper browns may not be as complementary with the graying hair, the greens, teals and rich reds add an extra dimension and create a stronger, more powerful palette.

COOL / LIGHT

Cools with ash hair and blue or green eyes often benefit from the addition of the pastel colors to the cool palette. Some of the coral-pinks can add just the right amount of warmth for a more youthful look, especially in the blushes. The variety of blues, especially the periwinkle colors and blue-greens, offer more variety and interest.

COOL / BRIGHT

The Cool with silver gray hair, blue or blue-green eyes often benefits from adding some of the bright colors to her cool palette. The clear bright blues, turquoises and coral-pinks add strength without heaviness and often give the cool palette more life. A true Cool with dark ash hair and hazel eyes often prefers stronger colors. She may find the deep too dark and heavy. The bright adds just enough contrast for additional strength and to complement a more dramatic personality.

COOL / MUTED

The Cool with a hazel eye and ash hair color often has just enough warmth to her skintone that the addition of some of the muted colors teal, cocoa, grayed-green can add a new dimension to the cool palette while still maintaining the softness that is projected in the cool palette. Many Cools like the warm tones that are not complementary to their overall coloring. Adding some muted colors adds some warmth that is subtle enough not to become overpowering.

PART VIII
A WARDROBE PLAN

Now that you know the definition of a well-dressed woman and have the tools to develop your personal style, a few helpful hints can save you hours as you plan your wardrobe:

Where to Start

Most people are so busy running around that they do not have a good grasp of who or where they are. Pick up a pen and paper and map out the following for yourself.

1. *List your activities* over the space of a month or two and work out a rough percentage of time per activity.

WARDROBE COST-PER-WEARING FORMULA

Cost-per-wearing formula: This simple formula allows you to determine the true cost of a garment by dividing the purchase price by the anticipated number of wearings to arrive at a cost-per-wearing amount. Here is how to figure a cost-per-wearing value:

Let's say you buy a dress for $100 that you wear once every two weeks for 26 wearings. Divide 100 by 26 and your formula will look like this:

$$\frac{\$100}{26} = \$3.84 \text{ per wearing}$$

Compare this with an evening gown costing $150 and worn 5 times. The formula would look like this:

$$\frac{\$150}{5} = \$30.00 \text{ per wearing}$$

The best clothes you buy are the ones that make you feel fantastic because they are worn the most. The cost of a garment is less relevant to the amount paid than it is to the number of times it is worn. The more times you wear a garment, the cheaper it becomes. Work out a break-even price for the garment and when you reach it, retire the garment to a recycling or consignment shop.

Now go to your wardrobe and assess whether the percentage of clothes suitable for each of your activities relates to the *time* percentages.

GARMENT/ITEM	% OF DAY	GARMENT/ITEM	% OF DAY
1.		11.	
2.		12.	
3.		13.	
4.		14.	
5.		15.	
6.		16.	
7.		17.	
8.		18.	
9.		19.	
10.		20.	

In most cases, there is an imbalance, which is why we say "I have nothing to wear!" What we are actually saying is, "I have nothing appropriate to wear." This situation is most common among women entering or leaving the work force.

If you constantly undergo change in your life, you must repeat this exercise every six months or so.

2. Visualize the image you wish to convey to the world—one that is in keeping with your personality and life style. You may wish to change this image every so often.

3. Assess how much time you have to shop, dress and care for your clothes. If this time is highly limited, serious consideration must be given to your choice of fabrics, and the location of stores and shops.

4. How much money do you have for your wardrobe? Whatever your status, you should work out a realistic budget for each fashion season and stick to it. You can have fun getting maximum value and outfits from your budget, however small it is.

If you don't know how to do a clothing budget, the easiest way is to dig out the clothes, shoes, accessories, etc. bought last season and roughly add up the cost of each item. Then add between 10 and 15 percent to determine this season's budget.

5. Consider the climate in which you live or may be moving to, and think about the weights of fabric appropriate for this climate. (Many people do not appreciate the wind-chill factor in certain locations.)

6. Set yourself some positive goals for your appearance and your wardrobe. These following questions may help you to do this:

- Do you get regular compliments on the way you look?
- Are you buying the best clothing you can afford?
- Do you look and feel feminine in your clothes?
- Are you aware of the current fashion themes and colors?

Organizing Your Wardrobe

Most wardrobes and chests of drawers are cluttered with clothes that are no longer in service. A wardrobe that works is one in which every item can clearly be seen, and all items are for current wear.

You must set aside time to go through every item that's part of your wardrobe, hold it up and assess its viability in being there. Divide your bed into three sections—DEFINITELY IN, DEFINITELY OUT, and I DON'T KNOW, and then sort through everything.

Do not put the I DON'T KNOWS back into your main wardrobe. Store them in a case, a box or on a high shelf and see how often you go to them. Chances are you never will, so after a few months give them away or throw them out. Before getting rid of clothes, see if you have any good enough to be recycled at one of the many clothing consignment stores. The proliferation of these shops means that it is no longer necessary to keep clothes until they are worn out. The money you get back can go towards next season's garments.

To achieve a wardrobe in which all items are for current wear, remove:

- "Fat" or "thin" clothes if you fluctuate in weight.
- Anything not worn over the past year.
- Clothing that needs repair or is unwearable for any reason.
- Out-of-season clothes.
- Outdated clothes.

Unless you have a large hanging area, it is wiser to store out-of-season clothes in boxes, suitcases or other convenient spots. On unseasonably chilly days, layer clothes for extra warmth.

Good, sturdy hangers are essential in avoiding repeat ironing, and you must have proper hangers for skirts and pants. **NEVER** hang one garment over the top of another as it causes creasing and makes clothes hard to find. There should be at least 1-inch of space between each of your hangers to allow clothes to breathe and avoid creasing.

Hang similar items together in a long and short format if you have only one pole: coats (long), blouses (short), dresses (long), jackets (short), pants (long), etc. New closet organizing kits are available that allow for double poles where short items (blouses, jackets, etc.) can be hung one above the other.

Separate suits, put the jacket with your other jackets and the skirt with other skirts. By doing this, you will discover combinations for outfits you never realized you had.

SHOES are an expensive part of your wardrobe and should be stored properly and maintained regularly. Here are a few tips:

- Store on a shoe rack, in labeled boxes, or in hanging pockets.
- When buying shoes, buy the correct cleaning agent at the same time.
- Always clean new shoes and bags with neutral polish before wearing or using them, as they are not often properly waterproofed. This also protects them from scuffing.
- Repair nicks and grazes in shoes with nail glue, then color over with a felt pen and then seal with neutral shoe polish.

Integrated Wardrobe Plan

There is a simple and extremely effective way to reduce your expenditure each fashion season and at the same time get more outfits than ever before. The basis of this plan: your choice of colors.

Instead of buying a wide range of the new season's colors, choose just THREE that work together and look wonderful on you. These colors can then be supplemented with neutrals to build a spectacular wardrobe. Your selection of colors is much easier if you have had a personal color analysis, as your best colors are highlighted and your neutrals defined.

If you have some good clothes left from the previous season, check to see if the colors will go with some of the new shades, so that your combinations have a fresh new look. Use the Always In Style Portfolio for ideas on new shades and combinations.

Using the Basic Wardrobe Chart on the following pages, work out an exact list of your requirements and then buy clothes in your chosen color scheme. Additional bright colors can be added, but only for smaller items and accessories. Multicolored prints are fine as long as some of your chosen colors appear in the design.

When choosing your colors, think of the image that you wish to present to the world and make sure that the colors complement this image. Remember that colors evoke strong emotional feelings and must be appropriate for the occasion as well as for your personality.

It is wise to choose fairly simple styles for the main garments in your survival wardrobe, because they are easier to mix and match, and to accessorize. Buy garments that are versatile and can be worn for several occasions by being dressed up or down. Treat each item of clothing as a separate garment (e.g., think of a suit as a jacket and skirt).

Vary the weights and textures of your garments to be able to adapt to changes in temperature. Make use of layering for temperature control. If buying a coat in colder regions, make sure that it fits over all your garments.

No matter what color scheme you have chosen, it is wise to always include a white blouse to create a crisp look. This can be pure white, ivory, soft or creamy white, according to your coloring.

Only buy clothes and styles that you know will complement your coloring, body line, personality and lifestyle, or you may look as if you are wearing someone else's clothes.

The well-dressed woman is one who wears clothes that:

- complement her physically,
- express her individual personality,
- are appropriate for the occasion, and
- reflect the current trends.

If you have problems in knowing what suits you, consider attending one of our Always In Style courses, which covers each of these aspects in detail.

Basic Wardrobe Chart

In order to maintain balance and harmony in your survival wardrobe, select individual pieces with the same or similar details and silhouette lines to complement your body lines, i.e., straight, soft-straight, or curved. Wardrobe plans for body lines are pictured in the Always In Style Portfolio each fashion season.

Jacket (can be suit jacket)
- solid neutral color
- classic style in your line
- matching buttons or no buttons
- natural or quality blend fabric
- quality tailoring

Good Skirt
- to match jacket, above, or
- can be contrasting neutral, solid, tweed, herringbone, or check

Pants
- solid neutral
- quality fabric and tailoring

First Blouse
- white, soft white, ivory, or oyster
- simple style

Second Blouse
- any solid color
- print or pattern
- front button for use as overblouse

Third Blouse
- solid color
- dressier style and fabric

Two Sweaters/or Knit Tops
- basic color
- cardigan style will work as jacket
- crew, cowl, V, turtle-neck
- cotton knit in summer

Dress I
- solid color
- simple style for day or night
- minimum detail
- long sleeve

Dress II
- two-piece
- print or pattern

After-5 Pants, Skirt, Dress
- basic color for pants or skirt
- any color from palette for dress
- dressy fabric for dress

Casual Pants, Skirts, and Tops
- fun colors or prints
- casual fabrics

Coat
- neutral color
- quality fabric and tailoring
- simple classic style in your line
- matching buttons
- may be all-weather coat

Casual Coat
- can be jacket or parka
- slicker, wool, leather
- neutral or bright color
- cotton jacket in summer

Evening Dress
- any color
- only buy if necessary
- two-piece is more versatile
- may add pants

Essential Accessories
- smart day shoes in neutral color, pump or sling-back
- flat or sport shoe
- bag
- evening shoes and bag
- good walking shoes, tennis or jogging shoes
- boots in winter
- 3 scarves
- earrings
- bracelet
- necklace

To your survival wardrobe you can add any extra items necessary for your individual life style. If using clothes from a previous season, you MUST update where necessary by adjusting lengths, shoulders and accessories as shown in the Always In Style Portfolio.

Shopping Efficiently

Having cleaned out your closets and dressers and sorted your clothes, you should be able to jot down what you already have for this season's Basic Wardrobe. There will be obvious gaps on your chart, and these form the basis of your shopping list. Once you have purchased your main requirements, any money left over in your budget can be used for fun buys or accessories.

Shop at the start of each fashion season, when there is the widest selection of clothing to choose from. Most designers plan a total range of coordinates, which shoppers then pick the eyes out of. If you wait too long, there will be nothing left to go with the skirt, jacket, etc. you wish to buy.

Best times to shop are mornings and early in the week, when you, and the stores are not rushed. Do not take children with you when you are seriously shopping for clothes.

Dress well, and wear make-up and hosiery when shopping for clothes as you will get more respect from sales staff and look much better in the changing room. Take appropriate shoes with you for the garment you are planning to buy.

Save time by finding a few shops that sell the type of clothing you like at prices you can afford. Then get to know the manager or leading salesperson and explain your likes and needs. Pop in every so often until they know you well, and can point you toward good buys.

Take note of the labels of designers and manufacturers that give you a good fit and suit your life style and complement your body line. Carry this list with your color swatches.

Invest, where possible, in natural fibers or quality blends that wear longer and look better.

Avoid impulse buying, and don't go to sales unless there is something specific that you are looking for. Sales buys often blow clothing budgets on useless garments. Good buys at sales are shoes and bags.

Be selective. You are far better off buying a few quality items than you are a wide range of mediocre peices. Follow the golden rule: *"Love it madly, need it badly, or don't buy it!"*

BUY, WEAR AND LIVE FOR TODAY—not for when you may need it, because too often that day never comes.

Wardrobe Plans for Every Body Line

Identifying your body line is the first step to developing your personal sense of style. Your body line is a combination of your face shape and your body shape. *Even if you gain or lose weight, your body line will never change* because it is determined by your bone structure and the way your flesh is arranged around your bones. Is your face angular or curved? Is your body straight or rounded? Notice in the illustrations below that clothing lines reflect body lines, with particular attention focused on neck and waistline detail. By selecting clothing and accessories that have the same or similar shape as your body line, you can feel confident that you are complementing your unique shape.

STRAIGHT

Your face has beautiful angles that are enhanced by straight shapes in necklines, earrings, and hairstyles. Your body line also projects a straight silhouette that is flattered by crisp, clean, tailored lines and geometric designs.

Look for:
- Crisp, straight closings
- Angular and asymmetrical details
- Well-defined shoulders
- Straight hemlines on jackets and skirts
- Little or no waist emphasis
- Tailored lines
- Angular earrings, buckles, bags
- Geometric patterning

See pages 146-7 for wardrobe

SOFT-STRAIGHT

Your face shape has lovely soft curves that are complemented by contoured earrings, hairstyles, and necklines with soft movement and shape. Your body line is less curved and thus projects a straighter line. Soften your neckline, shoulder, and bustline areas. Keep straight lines around your waist and hips for a longer, more slender silhouette.

Look for:
- Combinations of straight and smooth lines
- Soft lines around face
- Straighter silhouettes below bustline
- Unconstructed shapes that are neither all straight nor all curved
- Curved earrings, angular buckles
- Soft patterning around face

See pages 148-9 for wardrobe suggestions.

STRAIGHT-SOFT

Your face shape has well-defined angles that contrast beautifully with your curved body line, creating a sophisticated silhouette. Select straight geometric shapes for earrings, hairstyles, and neckline treatments. Soften your silhouette below your shoulder with waist emphasis or soft, flowing styles.

Look for:
- Combinations of straight and smooth lines
- Crisp, straight lines around face and shoulders
- Waist emphasis
- Fitted and wrapped shapes that are neither all straight nor all curved
- Angular earrings, contoured buckles and belts
- Geometric or abstract patterning

See pages 150-1 for wardrobe suggestions.

CURVED

Your face has soft, elegant curves that are repeated in the rounded contour of your body. Soften your hairstyle, necklines, and accessories with curved shapes. Use waist emphasis and soft, flowing styles in drapable fabrics to enhance your curves.

Look for:
- Smooth, sleek curves on closings and lapels
- Soft skirts
- Rounded hemlines
- Soft tailoring details
- Curved earrings, bags, buckles
- Soft patterning

See pages 152-3 for wardrobe suggestions.

Straight Body Line Wardrobe Plan

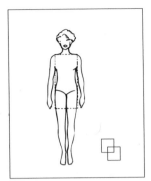

**ANGULAR FACE
STRAIGHT BODY**

If you have determined that your body line is straight, the following illustrations reflect the most complementary silhouettes for you based on this season's looks. These items are the basis of a flexible wardrobe plan from which a variety of outfits can be created. Use the ideas shown to help you combine items from your existing wardrobe in new and exciting ways or to assist you in selecting new pieces that enhance your body line and express your personal style.

Update straight body lines with:

- ❑ Slimmer, trimmer silhouettes
- ❑ A-line dresses and skirts
- ❑ Knit tops with straight side vents, v-necklines, notched polo collars, and ribs or geometric patterning
- ❑ Pin stripes, plaids, and checks
- ❑ Flat front narrow pants

C

D

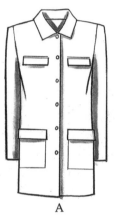

A

B

G

E

F

K

H

I

J

B+E+I   A+K   F+G+J   D+G+K   E+H

C+F+I   B+E+K   C+D+H   F+G+K   A+C+J

Soft-Straight Body Line Wardrobe Plan

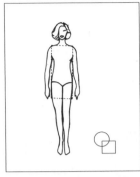

**CONTOURED FACE
STRAIGHT BODY**

If you have determined that your body line is soft-straight, the following illustrations reflect the most complementary silhouettes for you based on this season's looks. These items are the basis of a flexible wardrobe plan from which a variety of outfits can be created. Use the ideas shown to help you combine items from your existing wardrobe in new and exciting ways or to assist you in selecting new pieces that enhance your body line and express your personal style.

Update soft-straight body lines with:

- ❑ Slimmer, trimmer silhouettes
- ❑ Soft knit tops
- ❑ Tweeds
- ❑ Fur collar and cuff treatments
- ❑ Narrow pants
- ❑ A-line skirts

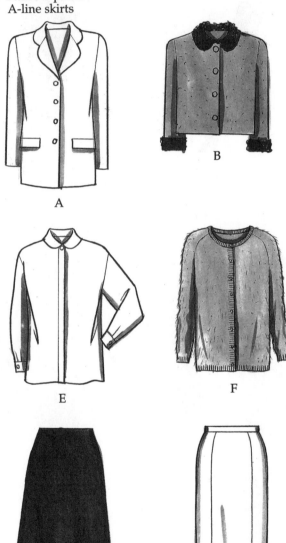

A

B

C

D

E

F

G

H

I

J

K

E+F+I   D+H   A+G+J   B+H   D+E+K

A+C+K   B+I   F+G+K   C+D+J   F+G+J

Straight-Soft Body Line Wardrobe Plan

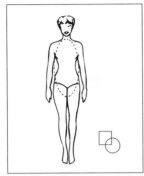

**ANGULAR FACE
CURVED BODY**

If you have determined that your body line is straight-soft, the following illustrations reflect the most complementary silhouettes for you based on this season's looks. These items are the basis of a flexible wardrobe plan from which a variety of outfits can be created. Use the ideas shown to help you combine items from your existing wardrobe in new and exciting ways or to assist you in selecting new pieces that enhance your body line and express your personal style.

Update straight-soft body lines with:
- ❏ Shaped and belted jackets
- ❏ Trench coats
- ❏ Asymmetric wrapped styles
- ❏ Gently flared skirts
- ❏ Full pleated trousers
- ❏ Shadow plaids and tweeds

C

A

B

G

D

E

F

H

I

J

K

A+C+J   B+E+K   F+G+J   A+G+K   E+H

B+C+I   F+G+K   D+C+H   F+E+I   D+C+K

Curved Body Line Wardrobe Plan

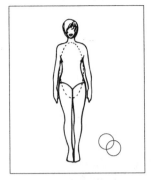

**CONTOURED FACE
CURVED BODY**

If you have determined that your body line is curved, the following illustrations reflect the most complementary silhouettes for you based on this season's looks. These items are the basis of a flexible wardrobe plan from which a variety of outfits can be created. Use the ideas shown to help you combine items from your existing wardrobe in new and exciting ways or to assist you in selecting new pieces that enhance your body line and express your personal style.

Update curved body lines with:
- ❑ Shaped and belted jackets
- ❑ Robe coats
- ❑ Fluid pants
- ❑ Flared skirts
- ❑ Fuzzy knits
- ❑ Princess line dresses and jackets
- ❑ Fur trims

C

D

A

B

G

E

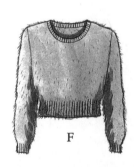

F

H

I

J

K

A+I   E+G+I   F+G+J   B+C+K   A+J

C+D+H   B+F+I   F+G+K   E+H   D+E+G+J

PART IX

HAIR AND MAKE-UP

It is often said that a woman's hair is her crowning glory. In fact, it is. A hair style and a color that complement her coloring and face shape, are appropriate for the occasion, enhance her personality, and are current and up-to-date fit our definition of the well-dressed woman.

Suggested Colors for Hair Color
- **Warm:** Medium in depth with golden or red highlights.
- **Cool:** Medium-to-deep color ranging from soft or ash brown to chestnut
- **Light:** Medium-to-light blonde or brown.
- **Bright:** Medium to dark in depth. From brown to a red titian color. Medium blonde often works with dark eyebrows and lashes.
- **Muted:** Medium in depth, ash blonde or brown. The darker the eye color, the lighter the hair can be.

Hair Styles
Hair styles should also complement the shape of your face and your body line.

Sharp-straight or **straight facial and body lines** call for an angular hair style, which can be created by:

- hair cut into a point in front of the ear,
- hair cut into a point in the nape area,
- hair bobbed off to create a straight-bottom design line,

- hair pulled back on sides creating a straight line,
- straight hair,
- curly hair cut into an angular silhouette, or
- straight edge bangs.

Soft-straight facial and body lines call for a hair style with a combination of straight and curly hair, or a style that is not obviously straight or curly. It can be created by:

- curly top and straight, short sides;
- asymmetrical style—straight on one side, curly on the other;
- slightly wavy hair; or
- smooth top, curly back.

Curved facial and body lines call for a curved hair style line, in the hair created by:

- curly hair,
- wavy hair,
- straight hair cut in a circular silhouette, or
- rounded lines in the nape area.

Make-Up

The picture of the well-dressed woman can only be completed by the perfect choice of make-up colors and their correct application.

Lipsticks

Cool: obviously blue based, rose tones. Look for names like:
Antique Rose,
Iced Azalea,
Plum Rose,
Azalea,
Wild Cranberry,
Raspberry Apple,
Dusty Rose,
Winter Fuchsia.

Bright: clear, true and bright reds. Look for names like:
Amaretto,
Bittersweet,
Apricotta,
Strawberry
Hot Red,
My Red,
Azalea,
Iced Azalea,
Zinnia.

Warm: burnished and golden. Look for names like:
Amaretto,
Cognac,
Mahogany,
Mango,
Apricotta,
French Brandy,
Nutmeg,
Spring Fling,
Bittersweet,
Terra Cotta.

Lipsticks

Muted: softened and neutralized. Look for names like:
Antique Rose,
French Brandy,
Terra Cotta,
Cognac,
Mauve,
Dusty Rose,
Mahogany.

Light: Rose to pink, soft. Look for names like:
Antique Rose,
Azalea,
Dusty Rose,
Mauve,
Spring Fling,
Bittersweet,
French Brandy,
Mango,
Iced Azalea,
Plum Rose.

Deep: rich and intense tones. Look for names like:
Hot Red,
Terra Cotta,
French Brandy,
Wild Cranberry,
My Red,
Winter Fuchsia.

Eye Shadows

Base/Highlights: Champagne, Soft Pink, Peach Glow

Accent and Colors:

Cool. Look for names like:
  Bright Sapphire,
  Smoky Grey,
  Dusty Plum,
  Stormy Blue,
  Sapphire Dust,
  Violetta.

Bright: Look for names like:
  Athens Blue,
  Sea Green,
  Bright Pine,
  Violetta,
  Bright Sapphire.

Warm. Look for names like:
  Athens Blue,
  Light Cocoa,
  Bisentine,
  Bright Pine,
  Light Sage,
  Irish Khaki,
  Sea Green.

Muted. Look for names like:
  Dusty Plum,
  Light Sage,
  Stormy Blue,
  Irish Khaki,
  Sapphire Dust,
  Light Cocoa,
  Smoky Grey.

Light. Look for names like:
    Athens Blue,
    Light Sage,
    Dusty Plum,
    Sea Green,
    Light Cocoa,
    Violette.

Deep. Look for names like:
    Bright Pine,
    Sapphire Dust,
    Bright Sapphire,
    Smoky Grey,
    Irish Khaki,
    Stormy Blue.

Blushers

Cool: obviously blue based, rose tones. Look for names like:
    Bright Clover,
    Soft Clover,
    Candied Apple,
    Tea Rose,
    Pink Shower.

Bright: clear, true and bright reds. Look for names like:
    Baby,
    Mango,
    Candied Apple,
    Coral Glow.

Warm: burnished and golden. Look for names like:
Apricot Tone,
Coral Glow,
Brandy,
Mango,
Cognac,
Nutmeg.

Muted: softened and neutralized. Look for names like:
Apricot Tone,
Soft Clover,
Brandy,
Tea Rose,
Cognac.

Light: rose to pink, soft. Look for names like:
Apricot Tone,
Coral Glow,
Brandy,
Mango,
Tea Rose,
Pink Shower.

Deep: rich and intense. Look for names like:
Candied Apple,
Soft Clover,
Cognac,
Baby,
Nutmeg.

Makeup Tool

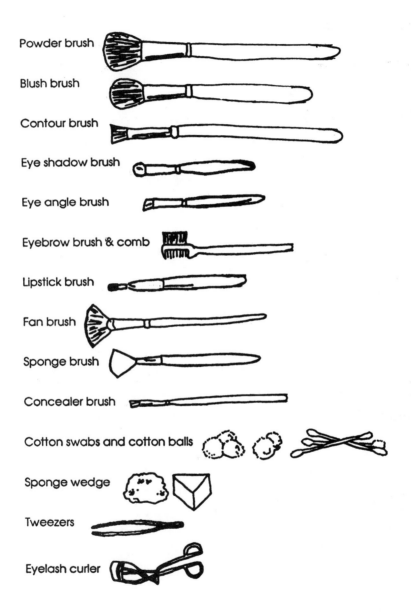

Powder brush

Blush brush

Contour brush

Eye shadow brush

Eye angle brush

Eyebrow brush & comb

Lipstick brush

Fan brush

Sponge brush

Concealer brush

Cotton swabs and cotton balls

Sponge wedge

Tweezers

Eyelash curler

Concealer

Concealer—Apply concealer in darkest part of recesses, frown lines, wrinkles. Blend with dampened sponge.

Light shadows and lines—Apply concealer over foundation.

Dark shadows and lines—Apply concealer under foundation.

sponge wedge

concealer brush

Corrector/Foundation

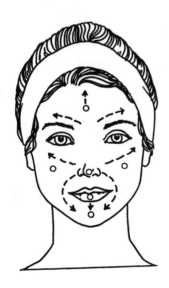

Corrector/Foundation—Dot on color corrector where needed. Then apply foundation. Blend the two together.

Corrector:
Ruddiness—Aqua tinted corrector tones down ruddiness.

Sallowness—Mauve tinted corrector clears up sallow skin.

Extra touch: Youth Radiance—For a lovely glow.

sponge brush

sponge wedge

Powder

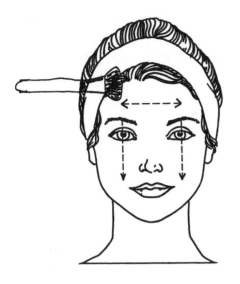

Powder:

1. Dip powder brush in loose powder, tap off excess powder.

2. Apply across forehead, then down over each eye and cheek.

3. Use fan brush to whisk away any excess powder.

powder brush

Blush

1. Apply blusher along top of cheek-bone, beginning under center of eye and smooth up and out into hairlines.

2. Do not bring blusher lower than an imaginary line from bottom of nose to just under ear. Placing blusher any lower can make your face appear to sag.

3. Dip contour brush in deeper-toned blush and dust in the hollow of the cheeks. Blend carefully.

blush brush

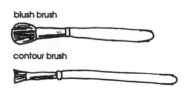

contour brush

Eyes

Eyeshadow Base

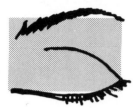

Sponge to blend

Eyeshadow Base—Apply base to entire eyelid area. Do not cover with foundation. This helps eyeshadow to stay set longer.

Eyebrows—To shape eyebrows, line up a pencil alongside nose. This is where the eyebrow should begin. Pivot pencil over center of eye to find the peak of your arch. Then pivot pencil to outer corner of eye for the end of brow. Pluck hairs or fill in with brow color if necessary.

Eyebrows

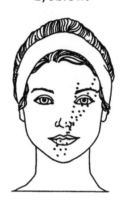

Eyeshadow 1

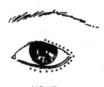

1. Highlighter

Eyeshadow brush

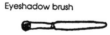

2. Liner

NO LID   AVERAGE LID   PROMINENT LID

Eye angle brush

Eyeshadow 2

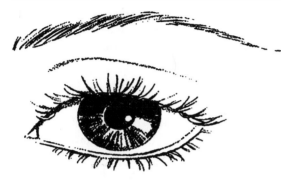

Eyeshadow II—
1. Highlighter—Lightest eyeshadow color is applied under eyebrow.
2. Liner (blend)—Along outer edge of eye and under eye.
3. Lid—Medium shade of eyeshadow to cover lid.
4. Orbital Bone—Deeper shade of eyeshadow in creases.

eyeshadow brush　　　eye angle brush

Mascara

Mascara—

brow and lash brush

Apply mascara to lower and upper lashes. Use lash comb to separate lashes.

Lipstick

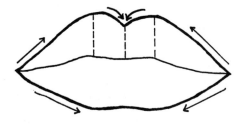

Lipstick brush

Lipstick brush

Lipstick—

Draw three vertical lines in center of lips with a lip pencil. Use lip pencil to outline lips, following arrows. Fill in with lipstick applied with lip brush.

The Outraged Woman

After each and every one of my color lectures during the past few years, there has always been one woman who objected violently to being limited to a single palette of colors. She often bordered on real hostility; mentally stamping her foot, she would defiantly assert, "I WILL WEAR ANY COLOR I WANT TO WEAR!" In retrospect, she was often the one person in the audience who always caught my eye because she made such a strong non-verbal impact through her fashion statement.

In the beginning we learned which lines, scales, prints, and textures of clothing are correct for our body type by looking at our face shape and body shape. Upon consideration of our personality, we expanded on this information to create a wardrobe that projects each of us as individuals. Just as we "added to" or "multiplied" information to attain our style, so should we determine our direction with colors to *complete* our style.

Our "outraged" woman wants to wear any—and every—color. She understands, perhaps, that some colors look better on her than others, but does not want to be limited to a palette, or to a flow chart. She feels that she is justified, through her strong desire and conviction, to wear any color, especially the fashion colors.

Grand Finale or
Just the Beginning

Following the tremendous success and popularity of color analysis in recent years, some people have been concerned about looking like part of a group. I began to notice that instead of compliments about how wonderful I looked in my colors, I was hearing comments like "you must be an Autumn."

Now all this has changed. Not since the early days of teaching those first color classes have I felt such excitement. The complements are once again "how wonderful you look!" -- not just how great I look in my colors. The difference: being able to look fabulous by expressing who you in a correct, and thus complementary, way.

All of my original color clients are selecting the color charts that will help them successfully expand their colors. New clients are identifying which color charts reflect their coloring and personality. Those who have the desire to reach further are learning ways to wear all colors, how to coordinate their new colors with their existing wardrobes, and how to create stunning, unique looks in order to fulfill their individual needs. Each one has her own personal style -- her own line, scale, and colors.

Let's take a final moment to reflect on the categories of style. Classic generally describes a formal, conservative style of dressing. Natural describes a less formal, more relaxed, casual style. Romantic describes a dressy, yet formal style. Dramatic describes an exaggeration of one of the three, whether it is formal, casual or dressy.

Now that you understand the times, places, and occasions when each style is appropriate—and understand your body line and personality—you know in which category (or categories) you are most comfortable. You're now ready to use this knowledge to expand your horizons. Only you know who you are, and who you want to become. I hope I have helped you span that bridge, regardless of its height and length, to be *Always in Style*.

Doris Pooser, Beauty and Style Expert Speaking Topics

Doris Pooser, a recognized expert in the fashion and beauty industry for over twenty years, has helped thousands of women and men to look and feel their best. In an entertaining and informative program, Doris has over 20 years of experience addressing these important topics:

- Image, Personal Style & Self Esteem
- Presentation Skills, Personal Packaging & Body Language
- Travel & Dining Etiquette
- Men & Women: Relationships in the Work Place, Wardrobe Essentials

Presentations will be focused and targeted to the needs of the client and may include some of the following titles:

- Successful Style
- The Secrets to Success
- Getting ahead in Business and your Personal Life
- Gaining the Competitive Edge
- Building Self Confidence
- Looking Good and Feeling Good
- The Women Entrepreneur/Women in Business

Whether it is climbing the corporate ladder, achieving success in your own business or improving your personal life, your image can make the difference between being average or exceptional.

It has been show that within the first 30 seconds that you meet someone they form an opinion about you.

- 55% is how you look
- 38% is your presentation: voice and body language
- 7% is what you have to say.

Your Personal Style can get you 93% of the way to making a positive first impression and unlocking the door to personal success.

Developing Personal Style improves:

- Self Esteem
- Confidence
- Credibility

Books:

- *Always In Style*: Color, Bodyline, Wardrobe and Image Building for Women
- *Successful Style*: Style for Men (Career Dressing, Body Language, Dining Etiquette, Presentations Skills)
- *Secrets of Style*
- *The Essential Guide to Hair, Makeup and Skincare*

Workshops are available with personal critiques, advice and recommendations for each attendee. For information on personal advice or seminars go to www.alwaysinstyle.com .

INDEX